CHECKLIST
FOR BETTER TENNIS

1. Always cover
all shots —
by
Bisecting angle
open to you

A compilation of coaching tips for the intermediate tennis player. The suggestions are paragraphed into a step-by-step sequence for each stroke from service to lob. Each sequence is then further condensed into short, itemized CHECKLISTS at the back of the book which can be memorized and applied by each player during practice.

CHECKLIST
FOR BETTER TENNIS

William Bockus

Dolphin Books
Doubleday & Company, Inc.
Garden City, New York
1973

To Tom Pfaender

and

Harold Soukup

First Edition

ISBN: 0-385-04612-X
Library of Congress Catalog Card Number 72–97268

Contents

Introduction

This checklist is written for intermediate players. You are between thirty and ninety-five years old. (Oh, yes there are. I play doubles occasionally with a ninety-year-old who belts the hell out of the ball.) It is assumed you have been playing tennis for a number of years. You know how to score. You are aware of the umpteen kinds of grips. You know about the difference between fast courts and slow courts. You realize there must be some grass courts somewhere in the world, but you have never seen any. You have heard Uncle Bill tell about the time he was at Wimbledon in 1937 and saw Budge beat Hare, 12–10, or some such score in the final set, with Hare scrambling, sliding, fighting like mad to hold his service, while Budge would breeze through his, game-15, or game-30. You probably have two rackets. One old one, so you can play in the rain. Ten cents to a dollar you try to play Wednesday afternoons, Saturday mornings, and all day Sunday, if your spouse lets you. You are mildly irritated that the sport pages are always filled with pictures of football pileups, baseball pitchers, tall basketball players, and what this manager said about this manager, but not a thing about tennis except a two-inch box under "Cooking Hints" containing the Eastern Clay Court Championships result in print that requires a magnifying glass to decode.

"Do you know, Janet, there are ten million tennis players in the United States? People who really get out and PLAY the game. Not sitting on their duffs watching, but actually playing the game! You'd think the news guys would like to increase their sports page readership by ten million readers. For cryin' out loud!"

Your source of greatest irritation is that grinning "poop-shot" guy who always seems to win with chops, sloppy lobs, and rinky-dink drop shots. A worse disappointment, however, is finding the public courts reserved all day Saturday and Sunday for a junior tennis tourney, or breaking a string at five o'clock Saturday afternoon. And with these new-fangled metal rackets you can't even drive a matchstick in the holes to hold the gut until Monday. Your greatest thrill is NOT winning third place in mixed doubles . . . it is opening up a can of new tennis balls.

This book is NOT for beginners. A beginner would be overwhelmed by the number and variety of suggestions given here concerning the game. A beginner should be given a few simple suggestions to work out over a period of weeks, usually by someone competent to judge not only what basics should be emphasized, but experienced enough to recognize the individual differences in pupils. Some kids just want to play for a while first, their own way. Others can take the more formal way of set lessons on backswing, follow-through, etc. Some have natural strokes; others need loads of help. There are always those adults who love to play tennis so much that they can't understand that some children would rather be mechanics or veterinarians during their free play time. And there is no better way to kill the desire to play tennis in children than to push or force them into a rigid set of detailed lessons week after week if they don't want it.

This book IS for the player who rarely gets coaching; who cannot practice four hours every day; who does have a fair game; who finds some spare time now that the kids are getting older; and who has that insane desire to beat everyone 6–0.

NOTE: If this book IS used by a beginner in lieu of a coach, he should heed the instructions in the section "Coaching." At the start it is very important to limit yourself and your partner to, say, two or three basic checklist items and let your natural abilities work for you before you try refining the strokes. Most people have a lot of natural ability, and this takes time to develop, as in any discipline. I would urge you very strongly to play for forty or fifty hours before adding other checklist items.

PURPOSE

The purpose of this book is to act as a reminder. It is an organized compilation of all suggestions I can remember over a period of forty-five years playing tennis as a duffer. I have listed these in the form of condensed checklists in bold print at the back of the book, which you can glance over quickly before practice. Or you can study the more complete explanations in the paragraphs at the front of the book.

It does not tell you what grip, or style, or stroke, or tactic is best for you. YOU have to make that choice. The checklists merely restate in rather concise terms what you already know but PROBABLY DON'T PRACTICE INTENSELY. In the book, *Match Play and Spin of the Ball*, William Tilden emphasizes again and again the need for INTENSIVE practice. He implies that long hours of play or practice mean very little if there is indifferent concentration on details and no self-analysis. In other words, it is much better to practice fifteen minutes on one stroke in which you constantly think "checklist" before and after each stroke, than it is to practice three hours with a haphazard approach. In fact, practicing the "wrong" way actually limits your chance to improve by constantly reinforcing your poorest strokes as surely as it reinforces your better ones.

The divers on a university swim team used to fool around on the three-meter board every now and then with comic diving: legs and arms akimbo, water spurting out of the mouth, sliding off the end of the board as if they had slipped, etc., the whole bit. But just let the coach come upon that scene and it was, "Stop that! Don't you know that every time you make your approach and hurdle the wrong way, it takes you that much longer to learn the grooved approach? Come on now, let's get with it." His point could be well taken by most tennis players who want to improve. You only have a limited time for practice, and if you don't take advantage of every second, you are not only wasting your time, you are probably getting worse by setting up habits on your "comic" strokes that have become so ingrained you'll never be able to correct them without intensive effort.

Usually players already know the suggestions in these check-

1

lists, but they have to learn to remind themselves WHEN THEY ARE STROKING. And they must learn to do it INTENSELY, that is, EVERY time they make that stroke, until the stroke becomes as natural as throwing a ball or riding a bicycle. Just thinking about playing better tennis and then playing Saturday or Wednesday afternoon in the same old way helps not one iota. Even champions keep trying to improve the weakest parts of their games. They even return to old coaches to find out what is going wrong with a stroke. They practice intensely. They think and they analyze, because they want to play better tennis. They don't just dream about it.

To get the most out of the two hundred or so suggestions reiterated in this book, go over the checklists and mark a few items in each that you feel you need intensive work on. Then memorize the sentence below and follow its advice each time you play or practice:

Forget the score and think "checklist" before and after each stroke until the stroke becomes a habit as natural as throwing a ball or riding a bicycle.

You are apt to say, "Well, there's a lot more to tennis than strokes." Possibly, but stroke can be interpreted to mean anticipation, approach, footwork, targeting, swing, and follow-through as well as just swinging the racket.

Look at it this way. A coach can point out your weak areas and give you constructive criticism. But once you understand the suggestions he CANNOT practice for you. Most of us are lucky if we can afford even a few lessons from a good coach—and, at that, he does not follow us around afterward reminding us. So in about two months we are often back to our old habits WITHOUT EVEN REALIZING IT. We glean most of our information from friends, possibly high school or college team members, books on tennis, magazine articles, or just by trying different things. The recent tennis tournaments on TV are somewhat helpful. But the picture is so small and the action so fast that even an advanced intermediate learns very little from it. However, if we are asked how to describe a few of the things to consider during serv-

2

ice, for example, most of us could come up with some fairly reasonable answers. In fact, it is a lot easier to TELL someone how to serve, than it is to demonstrate a good serve. Right? Of course right!

There is an old saying that goes something like this: "People over thirty don't have to be educated, but they do have to be reminded." Another one: "Within one year you forget 90 percent of what you hear and 75 percent of what you see." And one more (with a grin, of course): "Dammit, don't do as I do. Do as I say!"

Our capacity to memorize and then recall a visual image is more efficient for most of us than our ability to remember and recall verbal instructions. Therefore a number of small drawings are placed beside items in this checklist wherever possible. Just before you go out to play or practice, glance over the items that you choose to concentrate on that day. Impress the words AND the drawings or diagrams that accompany the suggestions on your mind.

As you play, reserve a moment just before you start your action to recall the three or four suggestions or drawings. (Oh, yes you can.) After the stroke use a split second to analyze your action: What was it you did NOT accomplish? And keep this procedure up with EVERY stroke, until you feel your stroke has become as simple and unconscious for you as throwing a ball or riding that bicycle. A dedicated player can very easily memorize and recall, say, five or six suggestions on service (he has plenty of time to think before each serve), and certainly three or four items for each of the other strokes. Many of the suggestions will overlap, such as "Early backswing" or "Eyes on contact point AFTER impact," so it does not necessarily become a difficult memory problem. The difficult part will come in constantly forcing yourself to recall the items on EVERY stroke. How easy it is to think you're going to watch the ball impact the strings . . . and upon analysis, discover you can't remember whether you really did see the racket head on the last two strokes. INTENSITY of recall on EVERY shot is the key to a better game. After you accomplish one suggestion to your satisfaction, then add another, until you feel all of your

3

selected checklist items have become an unconscious part of your game.

NOTE: The above is not recommended procedure for tournament play. During a tournament it is probably better if you use the strokes you have without analyzing them too much, and instead concentrate mainly upon tactics and over-all strategy.

Now, what did we mean by that "forget the score" bit in the sentence you were supposed to memorize? Well, let's say you're playing doubles, and the score is 30–40, and you are serving. If you are really conscious of that score, you will probably return immediately to your old patty-cake serve, because you feel you just HAVE to get it in. A double fault at this moment is disastrous. So out the window goes the checklist, all your good intentions, and you get across your old reliable double-slick twist floater . . . which the opponent promptly pulverizes. You have saved face. (You did not double fault.) Your partner is not glaring at you. The opponent is happy, "Man, what a return!" However, you have interrupted your intensive practice. You practiced the patsy serve once again and in so doing probably knocked out all the learning of the previous six services. The point is: Do you really want to become a better player, or do you want to placate your partners? Do you really think you can go back to your old way of playing in the pinches, reinforce the incorrect habits, and still expect your synapses to become better relays? Well, I'll tell you. You can't.

Now, suppose you had said to yourself instead, "To hell with the score. I'm going to learn to serve in the pinch as well as in practice. Let's see how good I am." And you let go with a three-quarter-speed bomber to his backhand corner. It's out by a foot. So you let one go at half speed. It's in by a foot and bounces high to his backhand. He muffs it. It's deuce again, and you've got four more tries at service coming. You are walking on air. You are confident. You'll never use that stupid double-slick twist floater again. As psychologists point out, if you can break a habit just ONCE, you have a much greater chance of breaking it the second time, and so on, on a logarithmic scale. So "forget the score" means to continue your intensive practice regardless of the score. Keep score, but don't let it keep you.

And persevere.

Tennis is a rigorous discipline. You are moving; the ball is moving; the opponent is moving. You must control the ball with a "stick," not your hands. The area of placement changes from shot to shot, and the space through which you must send the ball is restricted by a net. In other words, "It ain't easy."

A rough relative idea of the time it takes for a dedicated player to improve his strokes markedly, or discipline his game to where he is one or two points better per game, to where he has confidence and power in strokes that are almost habitual, is as follows:

	Practicing 3 or more hours per day, 6 days per week.	*Practicing 1 or 2 hours per day, 3 days per week.*
High athletic coordination	6 months	2 years
Average coordination	1 year	4 years

With the above in mind, then, set your objectives realistically. The way most of us play, say, two or three times per week, it will probably take a good year before you really notice that your confidence is getting better and your game is getting tougher. But in that year you will notice plateaus of improvement. Suddenly you realize that you haven't worried about your second service going in for over a week. Aha, now let's see if I can add a little more power. What does the checklist say about power? Or can I reason it out myself? Also, in that same period, you will be having more fun. With concentration on early backswing, the game seems to have become easier. You seem to have loads of time, and you get more satisfaction out of really leaning into 'em, instead of dabbing frantically at the last moment. Now it may be that the resultant drives you are letting loose are sailing out or grabbing the net cord. You may even be losing MORE

5

points than you did with your old "safe" floater shots. But if you have any tennis sense at all, you will keep on with the intensive (check before and check after) pattern of stroking. Because once you start getting your weight and shoulder into the shot early, the second step, CONTROL, will come along just as surely. And all of a sudden you are holding them in the court, and the opponents are the ones who are dabbing frantically, leaning back over their baseline, wondering, "Where did she learn to hit 'em like that all of a sudden?" Little do they realize that "All of a sudden" happened because of one whole year's concentration on details and INTENSIVE practice.

So don't give up too soon.

In the chart below, the dotted line is the typical level of play of most intermediates over a long period of time. The solid line represents a typical level of play by an intermediate who is trying to improve his game by CHANGING his old habits. Each downslide is usually caused by the introduction of new items from the player's checklists.

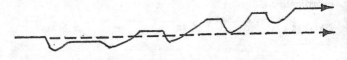

Chart

The upswings to a higher level of play usually come after the new items are integrated into his game. This plateau is maintained then until other items are introduced, during which his game is apt to suffer again.

Thus, particularly in tennis, any attempt by you to improve your strokes will probably result in a lower level of performance until your new habits are established. It is during this period that most intermediates give up and go back to their old "safe" patty cake. Consciously or unconsciously, they expect a miracle. "You know, Mabel, I've tried keeping that elbow and wrist firm on the backhand for THREE weeks, and it's worse than ever. I'm just going to keep running around them, I guess." She plays twice a week for about 1½ hours each time. The three weeks then add up to a total of nine hours of play, with the backhand stroke occupying, at the most, perhaps an hour of that time. One wonders how much of a song she could play on the piano with a one-hour lesson. How much of a cook would she be with one hour of instruction? The most intelligent people often seem to have no concept of real practice time. They may have the maturity to have long-term goals in everything else they do, but in tennis they continue to watch the game score like timid rabbits instead of shooting for the match score at the end of the summer!

Set your sights for a year from now.

Granted you may find it difficult to follow the instructions or suggestions in your selected checklists every stroke. Opposing players don't send you a waist-high bounce, four feet out of the side every time. You will still be overrunning the ball, fanning at bounces around your ankles, reaching way out in front with your shovel shot to pick up a plopper, etc. But even so, if you set up the habit of recalling the checklist items ("Backswing early"; "Pivot shoulders"; "Lock head"; "Lean into front bent knee," etc.) each time you go into action, you constantly REINFORCE the idea and gradually substitute a pattern of mental and muscular control in place of the old, unthinking, uncoordinated effort. A check on yourself is the only way to improve when you can't afford a coach. Most of us do not have instant reflexes and top-notch coordination, but we can LEARN to be pretty good tennis players by intensive mental and physical practice. If you commit the right habits to memory you will gradually discover you are not overrunning the ball as often; the balls that used to tangle in your ankles have begun to land out to one side; and the shovel stroke you used to employ for those drop shots has all but disappeared, because you watch the ball come off the opponent's racket, anticipate better, start sooner, and get the racket back half a second earlier.

The items in this book are suggestions. They are not necessarily the whole truth or the ONLY way to play. They were meant for you to read over and think about. Then adapt those items you think apply to your own game and your own physique. If you have a better way, great. Write your own items in the condensed checklists at the back of the book.

And if you do this, note that the items for each stroke are written in the order that they occur during the stroke and place your own suggestions within that sequence as precisely as possible. This makes the checklist easier to recall. For example, "Watch ball come off opponent's racket" is listed ahead of "Start backswing early." And "Lock wrist" comes before "Contact ball ahead of torso," followed by "Keep eyes on contact point for a split second AFTER impact," etc. Also note that each item in the condensed checklists at the back of the book has a number that is keyed to a similar number in the more comprehensive body of the text at the front of the book for that particular stroke. The shorter items at the back of the book are easier to memorize and recall than whole paragraphs of information, and recalling three or four of them just before each stroke can help immensely with the idea of INTENSIVE practice.

Read the PARAGRAPHS at your leisure, but memorize your CHECKLIST items just before you play.

SERVICE

There are several kinds of serves.

Regular:	Moderate topspin
Twist:	Maximum topspin
Flat:	Minimum topspin
Slice:	Sidespin
Underhand:	Usually backspin

REGULAR SERVICE

Note whether opponent is right- or left-handed.
Check wind direction and force.

1. Place your feet consistently.
   Serving to the deuce court, a basic position is as follows:
   Left foot pointed toward baseline at approximately forty-five degrees. (Do not touch baseline—foot fault.) Toe of right foot about twelve inches back of and approximately even with heel of left foot, with right foot approximately parallel to baseline. Keeping the right foot in this position (see Diagram A) helps ensure that you keep left shoulder pointing toward your aiming point.

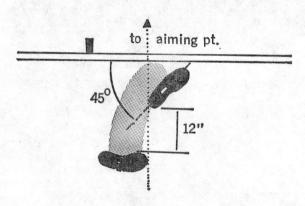

Diagram A

As you serve, the pointed left toe then allows the left heel to rise, which tends to give a few more inches lift to topspin action. Serving over a left foot that is perpendicular to a line drawn to your aiming point gives no lift. (Note Jimmy Connors' foot position on service.)

Serving to the advantage court, a basic position is as follows:

Left foot pointed toward baseline at approximately twenty degrees. Toe of right foot should be in same relative position to left foot as above. In other words, you merely turn your stance about twenty degrees clock-wise so that the line drawn from the right toe through the left heel points at your advantage-court aiming point (see Diagram B).

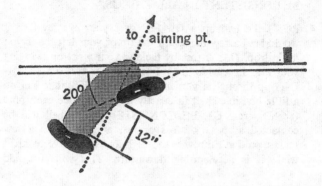

to aiming pt.

20°

12″

Diagram B

2. Keep shoulders somewhat parallel with line drawn between feet. Sometimes there is a creeping tendency, as you get fatigued, to turn the torso more toward the net with each progressive service until eventually your service becomes "flat" without much topspin and starts landing long. Before each serve push your left shoulder slightly to your right and forward. This will remind you that you should serve "sort of" over your left shoulder, and you will not wonder what happened to your service halfway through the third set if you use some gimmick like this for a reminder. (The gray areas in the two diagrams above represent the general shoulder position at the start of the serve.)

3. Use some rhythmical start for each serve, such as bouncing the ball once or twice. Hold one or two balls on first service. Holding one leaves the left hand free, or if you fault, forces a pause (during which time you may want to change foot position or some other item) while you dig the other ball out of your pocket. Holding two balls lets you go more rhythmically into the second serve, if you fault, but leaves you holding the extra ball if the

first service goes in. (Some players toss the extra ball behind them to leave the left hand free for emergency block volleys, two-handed backhands, etc.) Take your choice. But once you have made the choice, stick with it. BE CONSISTENT IN ALL THINGS.

4. PUSH the ball up a few feet over your eye level so it would land a few inches off the tip of your left toe if you let it drop. (Don't toss by flicking your wrist or swinging your arm in a wide arc.) Imagine your forearm PUSH-ING up through a vertical pipe as you SET that ball on a little invisible shelf in exactly the same place each time (see Diagram C). BE CONSISTENT. The ball will be contacted at peak of toss or just after it drops a few inches, so don't throw it too high and then have to hit it while it is accelerating downward. This will just add

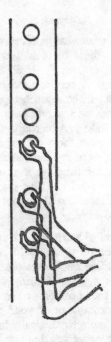

Diagram C

12

another variable and make it that much harder to have a consistent service.

As your left arm pushes that ball up, consider whether you want to start your weight moving back on to your right foot, so you can then transfer your weight forward onto the left leg as you come into your serve. Or you may want to start leaning forward as you push up your toss. Billie Jean King and Margaret Court are two players who lean forward into their serve as they toss. If you serve a modified twist serve you may stay rather stationary during the toss with arched back. Whatever your decision, do realize that this weight movement is a definite part of your serve DURING the toss. If you realize these items and remain consistent, then you are less apt to make errors.

5. Keep your eye on the ball, AND a split second after racket contact with ball, keep your eye on the contact point. In other words, don't look away at your opponent too soon. Head position is the key to torso action, just as in golf or diving, and if you move your head while you are serving it will cause the torso to move also (another variable).

> NOTE: You probably already have your grip for service established. Diagram D (looking at the butt of the handle) shows the angle between the face of the racket and the forearm of most service grips. Intermediates usually employ the grip "A," which has the forearm straight up and parallel with the racket face. Many top players use the grip labeled "B," like a modified backhand grip. You may find this angle uncomfortable at first, but in the long run it seems to give more topspin and drop IF you are serving and following through over that left shoulder.

6. In aiming the serve let the arc of your arm swing follow through toward the aiming point. Most of the time you want the ball to land in the backhand corner of the opponent's service court, but you must locate your AIMING POINT slightly to the right to compensate for the fact that the ball tends to curve to the left or carom

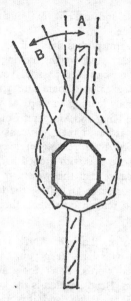

Diagram D

off the racket face to the left and ends up on the opponent's forehand. In the deuce court, for example, if your serves are landing five or six feet to the left of the divider line, change your aiming point until it is two feet to the RIGHT of the divider line. Even though you are now aiming your follow-through OUTSIDE the deuce court, the balls will curve or carom to your left and land one or two feet inside the backhand corner (see Diagram E).

During practice place a tennis ball can on the service line about two feet right of the deuce court. (Don't confuse the service line with the baseline.) Then serve by swinging your follow-through toward the can, and observe where your serves are landing. (You usually need about twenty serves to get an average unless you are an advanced player.) Adjust the can until the balls are landing in the backhand corner of the deuce court on target. Now REMEMBER the aiming point and USE

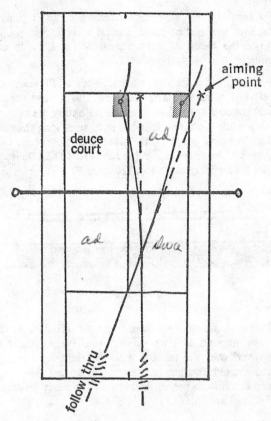

Diagram E

it. Yes, a few serves may drift over the divider line and go out to the right, but this is usually better than having 70 percent of your serves delivered to your opponent's best stroke, his forehand. (Always balance the fact that a few errors in good tactics are better than the many errors inherent in poor tactics.) Use the same adjustment system on the advantage court, and again, remember the spot!

A first serve to your opponent's wide forehand in the deuce court should be used more often than service to

15

forehand in the advantage court, because it pulls the receiver way out of court. Second serve should probably go to the backhand corner most of the time on either court.

7. For height aim through an imaginary SLIT about three feet above the net. The ball travels in a downward arc, and if you aim too low, you will be hitting the net or net cord much too often. It is better to serve long than short. The ball may curve in, the wind may blow it in, it may even hit the opponent, but a net ball is DEAD. Imagine that slit on every serve (see Diagram F).

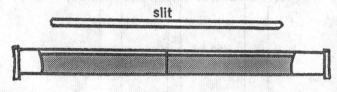

Diagram F

8. Weight is transferred from right to left foot as body rocks forward and up on left toe. Body usually falls forward over the left toe with the right leg coming up and around (during and after the stroke) for the first step toward the net or getting into the ready position on the baseline.

9. Legs may be straightened as contact is made with the ball. The entire action of a strong service is similar to a whip, starting with bent knees, mildly arched back, bent elbow with racket head almost scratching the back left shoulder, and ending with straight legs, balanced on left toe, body bent forward from hips, arm straight, and wrist snapped forward. (All of this often accompanied by a loud grunt, as the server tightens his diaphragm and stomach muscles.)

However, as one grows older, this type of action takes too much out of the server, and therefore many players don't straighten their legs particularly, or arch their back, but put more of their effort into the shoulder and wrist action to conserve their energy and vertebrae. Each person must judge his condition and desire in relation to his playing effort, both in time to be played and competition to be met, and then pace himself accordingly. And if you have a misplaced spinal disc or a trick shoulder, and your best effort is a flat hit from head height facing the net, then keep it. It is foolish to think you can practice a whiplash serve when you have a physical disability or you're in your late thirties or forties and only make it to the courts one or two days per week.

10. Fall forward over left toe in the direction of your aiming point. Do NOT fall sideways or back. Either of these latter movements will lose you force and control.

11. Racket strings meet the ball going primarily FORWARD and FLAT for just a few inches, with the top edge of the racket advancing upward (see Diagram G). Then the top right edge advances around and OVER the upper right side of the ball as the racket completes the stroke. (If this last topspin upward stroking motion is started too quickly, it often cancels out the forward force of the racket and causes a slower topspin service.)

Let the racket S-T-R-O-K-E that ball. SLING the ball toward that imaginary slit above the net. Use a LONG follow-through toward your aiming point. In other words, keep that right hand moving out as far as you can stretch during the wrist snap action. (Watch Stan Smith's follow-through on service.) Don't bring the right hand down across your body too soon. The critical period of control on any shot is that very short distance the ball is nestled on the strings of the racket. If you can insure that the ball is being propelled toward the aiming point during that period, you have it made. Anything you can do to come into the ball and leave the ball along that line of flight will make for positive control. You may even meet the ball a little too early or too late, but if the direction is right, the shot will be right.

Assuming similar coordination and reflexes, a tall man can contact the ball on service with arm completely ex-

Diagram G

tended. The shorter person may find it better to contact
the ball just BEFORE his arm is extended, since he gets
more rip up the back of the ball this way. The tall man
can get wrist snap forward, and maybe, in some cases,
down. The shorter person is not blessed with the extra
ten or twelve inches in height (tall men also tend to have
longer arms) that allow for a better angle and thus a
better chance of getting the ball in court. So the short
guy may have to rely on a little more topspin to make
up for his lack of height.

12. Get the ball moving toward that imaginary slit, three feet
over the net, FIRST. Then finish the whip action of
straightening elbow and wrist snap, which throws the
racket head forward and up. Wrist snap does not, on this
type of serve, mean bringing the head of the racket
down sharply. The final action of the wrist snap is akin

to the following: Take an old racket or a stick, cock it behind your shoulder with your elbow high, and then THROW it as if you were going to throw it over the housetop. Note that the impetus you give it is a force forward and UP, not forward and down. Use the same kinesthetic approach to your serve. Push the back of the ball forward and UP just AFTER you contact it with your flattish strings. Get it?

Actually the ball stays on the strings for a short time, and you need a certain attitude to serve well—firm and confident. A scared, nervous, short serving approach will never give you deep steady placements. Forget your game scores for six months and start serving firmly and confidently on ALL serves. You will note at the end of that time that your serves are starting to come in like boomers instead of dropping over the net like crippled ducks.

Use plenty of decisive wrist snap as the last motion of your stroke. After the ball leaves, the racket head will probably continue down and around your body and end up on the outside of your left leg. Power comes mainly from that wrist snap. A help to accentuate snap is to let the racket head dangle behind your left shoulder for just an instant before starting the wrist snap.

13. Rather hit both balls at three-quarter speed and get near the service court than slug wildly on the first one and then have to patty cake the second one. Also, you get twice the practice on one type of serve, and if you stay in rhythm you are much more apt to make the slight correction necessary on the second ball to bring it in.

As you begin to get a confident serve you will also begin to "feel" when you are hot. Service action, like many other physical activities, often runs in plateaus. Something happens, and everything starts falling together, both physically and psychologically. You just know about the middle of the first set that you've got that first service "grooved." When you feel that way, then stay steady and keep pounding them in. And remember this fact when your opponent gets a hot streak. Just grit your teeth and keep plugging away or change your game a bit to break his timing. Try a few chops, slices, or lobs. Even if he puts them away it may break his pattern, and sooner or later you start making points again.

Now, if it is YOU making the errors; if you are double faulting or sending your first service long, slow down a few seconds and THINK. Feet placement, shoulder nudge, accurate toss, push the first few inches FLAT toward aiming slit, then UP and forward on the decisive wrist snap, etc. If you've done your homework, your mind can run over your checklist in a few seconds. And probably just REMINDING yourself will get you back in the groove again.

14. If you do NOT follow service to the net in singles, get to the center of the baseline, come to a split stop (see "Retrieving" below), and watch the opponent's racket head in relation to the bounce. If the bounce is way in front of him he will tend to hit to your right. If the ball gets behind him, he will probably hit to your left, assuming your opponent is right-handed. (Intermediates usually do not move their feet fast enough to get their body opposite the ball. In other words, they don't really SCRAMBLE hard.)

15. If you DO follow service to the net in singles, run generally toward your opponent until he starts his stroke. Then come to a split stop on the BISECTOR (see "Approach Shots," Item 8 plus Diagram Q, for specific definition of bisector). As you watch his follow-through and determine where the ball is going and what kind of spin is on it, step into the ball (see "Volley" for details on stroke). Some players take very short, chopping steps and don't come to a full split stop. They just slow way down as the opponent strokes and then lean toward the incoming ball and use their forward motion to whip them out to the right or left for the volley.

RETRIEVING

Be a retriever. Take your hop, or rise on your toes and come down into your crouch with feet spread and knees bent. This is known as a "split stop." In other words, get that spring coiled and ready to shove off. Some players like to keep the right foot slightly to the rear of the left foot, so they can start forward as well as sideways. The top "retrievers" (those players who anticipate well and always seem to be able to get any ball back) often start their foot action WHILE the opponent strokes. It usually involves a short, quick shove off the right foot onto the left bent knee. Then if the ball comes to their right, the left knee uncoils and starts their body to the right. Or if the ball comes to their left, the left knee merely keeps bending and the right foot crosses over for a driving step to their left. And a one-step start is gold in the bank in tennis. Many intermediates, and especially the girls, do not realize that it takes as long to take the first step as it does to take the next TWO steps. In other words, once you get moving, keep going, because getting to the ball is a matter of acceleration, not constant speed. Too many players start indifferently for a wide ball and then stop, with a shrug, as if "I'd never have made it." What they fail to realize is that once they start accelerating they can cover the last ten feet to the ball in about the same time it took them to cover the first three or four feet! Another factor going for the alert retriever, and of which he is well aware, is that the ball may be coming in like an express train, but when it bounces it has to travel uphill, and old man gravity is hanging onto its tail like a ton of bricks. The ball slows down until it gets to the peak of the bounce and then, although it starts falling again, it has still a long way to go before it is dead. And that is where the retriever's racket usually catches it, about one foot off the ground, and sends it back leaving the opponent wondering, "How did he ever get his racket on that one?" So, kiddies, if you want a few extra points every few games, keep accelerating all the way. Even if you don't make it, the action has reinforced the good habits of anticipation, starting action, and early shoulder pivot with early backswing.

One last point: You will often find that when you do make a remarkable "save" you have a wide-open court or a great angle from the side to hit to. Now, a pro learns early never to count a "winner" until it hits the ground the second time, and he will follow every ball with the necessary defensive tactic and wait like a hawk for any miraculous return. But it is a different matter with the intermediate. He invariably loafs after a "put away" shot. Unconsciously he stands and admires his shot, and he is still admiring when your shot passes his wide open mouth and lands good. So keep accelerating!

Did you know that if you are chasing a ball way out to one side and you aim your return for the back part of the court, the ball does not have to pass over the net? In fact, if your shot is outside the net post the ball can travel BELOW net cord height and still be a good shot if it lands in court. Rule 22, c.

TWIST SERVICE

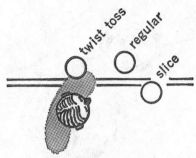

Diagram H

1. Push the toss up slightly lower and more over your head.

2. Arch your back more.

3. Emphasize the UP stroke, the wrist snap, and the straightening elbow to gain as much topspin as possible. But do not sacrifice all the forward motion of the racket head and hand. The forward motion is still necessary for direction. The stroke is like a whisk up the back of the ball and requires a very precise angle of attack. A characteristic error on this type of service is that the server sometimes hits the ball with the leading edge of the racket and sends it way up in the air.

4. Racket handle is almost parallel with ground when strings contact ball.

5. Weight transfer forward may help forward motion if service is too slow. Remember, however, that the twist service is a high arching ball, somewhat slower than the other serves, and thus gives the server more time to follow it to the net. So don't expect a fast ball from this delivery. Its PACE when it bounces will be fast enough and more than make up for its lazy-like approach.

6. Aim for that imaginary SLIT over the net, but this time place the slit four or five feet over the net, since you will have much greater drop.

Diagram I

7. Follow-through is rather short and off to the RIGHT of your body. The ball goes through the air with less SPEED than the regular or flat service, but it comes off the bounce with more PACE—fast and high. It usually veers to the server's right or the receiver's backhand. One of the nastiest serves to handle is the type of serve that lands slightly on the forehand side and takes off right at the receiver's head.

Since you will more likely be on the receiving end of twist services than serving them, consider the following: The incoming serve to your backhand takes longer to arrive, so you have an extra bit of time to run around it and take it on your forehand. If you really concentrate and anticipate you can do this fairly successfully. You will find that this type of ball looks like an inch-thick, flat, wobbling pancake as it approaches, and it is spinning like mad when it gets to your racket. So you must squeeze your grip extra hard and punch into the ball, with your shoulder and body behind it. If you stroke the ball your normal way it may twist the racket right in your grasp. Pros have such strong wrists and arms and powerful follow-throughs that they are not particularly bothered. The average intermediate often tends to panic or give up when he muffs the first six or seven returns of a twist service. So think, and start fighting back. If nothing else works, grab your racket with two hands, step CLOSER to the service line, and as the ball comes off the bounce get it on the rise with a semi-half-volley back and let it spin itself up into a lob. Or try coming into it hard with a chop block. You may suddenly discover an answer. And always remember, particularly if you are several rounds into a tournament, that this twist service takes an awful lot of energy out of the server to make it effective. In the second set you may find the server starting to drag. If so, start lobbing him and make him use that overhead stroke. Sometimes they have to quit using the twist and revert to a regular serve, which will help you a bit too. Many a match has been won after the first set was lost 0–6. Never quit!

NOTE: This twist type of serve is not recommended for long singles matches or even for the average intermediate player, and certainly not for middle-aged players. It is hard on the spine and sometimes lays up even a young player who uses it too much.

A mild form of this twist often makes a good second service. Use the suggestions above, but do most of the snap action with your arm and wrist and leave out the extremely arched back.

FLAT SERVICE

1. Use grip "A" in Diagram D.

2. Shift right foot around a bit so that a line drawn between the TOES of your shoes points at the aiming point.

3. Use as aiming point the place where you want to hit the ball. Aim direct, because there is very little curving right or left on a flat serve.

4. Push up the toss a bit higher and farther out in front than your regular serve. Say about two feet out in front of your left toe.

5. Stretch high on your stroke and try to get on top of the ball. Pretend it is looking down at you, and hit it flat on its forehead. If the top edge of your racket seems to push over the top and to the right a bit, let it. There is often some topspin on a flat serve, even though most of the power is directed at pounding the ball down in the opponent's court as hard as possible. The speed of the ball through the air is about the same as the pace of the ball after it bounces.

6. Aim again for that imaginary slit over the net. But this time lower it to about two feet over the net, since you will be getting less drop than with the regular serve. (This aiming for the SLIT is probably the most important item in the flat, hard serve. Cannonball servers, including the professionals, invariably make most of their faults on NETTED balls!)

7. Lean way forward when you contact ball.

8. Snap that wrist FORWARD, not down. The forward movement and forward-leaning angle of the racket face will give enough topspin to the ball to bring it in.

SLICE SERVICE

1. Change your aiming point more to the right than with the regular serve, because the ball tends to spin around a vertical axis and curves off the racket face more toward your left.

2. Feet may need some adjusting from your regular stance, such as moving your left toe farther to your right and even turning your shoulders more to your right.

3. Place your toss farther to your right (see Diagram H under "Twist Service").

4. Contact the ball more on its right side, away from you.

5. Lean into the stroke (toward the net) as in any other shot and make certain of the FORWARD motion of your racket head, so that all the force is not expended in slicing, which makes for a very slow ball.

A slice service, if hit moderately, makes a very reliable second service. In many cases it bounces differently depending on at what angle it contacts the surface of the court.

NOTE: This slice type of serve is often useful if the sun is right overhead, and you are one of those players who have trouble serving into the sun. Since the toss is slightly off to one side, you can look sideways at the ball and at least see it. It is better to be able to see your toss and get a moderately fast service in than to lose the ball in the sun and keep missing it.

UNDERHAND SERVES

The underhand serve was quite fashionable for the ladies when tennis was first introduced, but is rarely used today. However, some players who have nerve or muscular problems and cannot raise their arms or control an overhead delivery are still able to play by using this type of serve.

Use the same stance and start as a regular service.

There are four general kinds of underhand deliveries:

1. One starts by contacting the ball just below shoulder height, slightly ahead of the torso, using a chop action with plenty of forward motion. This results in an adequate service, because the ball is going downhill all the way and gathers speed as it goes. If hit deep into the court, it tends to skid on the bounce or at least stays rather low. Thus the receiver has to get low and hit up. However, if the ball is hit too short, and too easy, it sets itself up for a beautiful putaway by the receiver.

2. No. 2 starts by contacting the ball approximately two feet out in front of the left knee, using a slicing motion across the back face of the ball from right to left. This ball tends to go uphill and then down as it passes its peak (hopefully) a few feet in front of the net. The slice gives the ball a sidespin so that when it lands in the backhand corner it bounces toward the receiver's backhand. This is most effective when used in the advantage court, since it sometimes pulls the receiver way out to the side.

3. The third starts by standing behind the baseline in the position ready to hit a forehand drive. Feet are a little wider apart than regular service position, with left shoulder toward the net. The ball is set out in front of the left toe about three feet off the ground, and the racket comes through with a moderate forehand drive. The ball should be aimed for the backhand corner of the service court, as in any other serve. It needs topspin or it will tend to float long. Watch the ball until racket contact. Don't peek up.

4. The fourth starts with the standard approach to the regular serve. Racket starts back. Left hand starts toss. But

just as the left hand gets as high as your rib cage, and you are starting your weight transfer forward, set the ball out in front of your left knee about four feet out to the side and two feet off the ground. Bend your knees and come through the ball with a soft chop. Shoot to skim the net by about a foot, and drop it into the deep center part of the service court. It is better to hit this type of low chop right at the receiver rather than out to one side. Many intermediates hit a low- or medium-bounce ball fairly well, but if it comes right at them they rarely move their feet enough and try to handle it too close to their ankles.

There is another application of the No. 4 underhand serve above. It can be used in normal play as follows but probably should be used only in doubles and only on a first service to the advantage side. With your partner guarding the right-hand alley, come through the ball with the low soft chop but aim to drop it into the NEAR side of the advantage court as near the sideline as you can. This usually is effective only a few times during a match and only if you have been serving a hard first service. The receiver is expecting a fast ball and is often caught on his heels. In his rush to get this drop shot he almost always runs into it too hard and whales it out. Or if he is cagier he takes it on his backhand and invariably angles it across court just over the net to the other alley. (He has the option to lob, but since intermediates never lob, he probably won't in a pinch.) So remember the second part of this cat-and-mouse game: Just after you let go with the chop, take your regular two or three steps toward the open alley and get set to pounce in on his return angle shot. Even if you miss the serve you still have the second service left and no big loss except a few "wisecracks" from the other side of the net.

There are always those who complain that this serve isn't cricket. But let us look at an analogous situation in the Pacific Southwest Tournament last year. Two of the top professionals were playing a match near the end of the tournament. One of them, scrambling hard on a deep shot to his backhand, put up a high lob that fell at about the middle of the opponent's service court. The opponent got set for a put-away overhead. The other player got into his split stop position deep on his baseline. Just as the opponent was about to hit the overhead he stopped and drop-shotted the ball over the net. A round of applause, with BOTH players grinning—one with delight and the other with chagrin at being outfoxed. There is no USLTA rule that prescribes how you have to stroke. The rule on service only states that the ball must be hit before it reaches the ground. As long as your opponent is ready, anything goes.

Another instance of "no, no" tennis is the looping topspin drive. This went out of favor a number of years ago because of the emphasis on harder-hit straight drives. Now the looping topspin is being used again by pros. Watch Tom Okker's looping forehand, Tom Leonard's looping crosscourt two-handed backhand, or Bob Hewitt's wristy crosscourt backhand—if you can see them! Yet twenty years ago it was considered old-fashioned if you even looped your backswing. So always keep in mind that winning tennis is playing the best way you can and getting it back oftener than the other guy. Whether you play like Bobby Riggs or Don Budge, Pancho Segura or Pancho Gonzales, Arthur Ashe or Stan Smith, it doesn't matter much as long as you use your own talents to the utmost. If you like to drive, then drive like mad; if you're the foxier type who likes to employ a variety of strokes, then run 'em ragged left and right, up and back. But do it and don't listen to the complainers about what is "acceptable" tennis.

There are as many different kinds of services as there are people. And though there are many suggestions as to how to serve like a pro, we also have to be realistic and realize that most of us are not going to be of professional caliber. We are limited first by ability, second by desire, and third by practice time available. It is often more reasonable to correct a few of your worst faults: that eight-foot-high toss; that facing the net as you serve; that skip hop before you wind up; that stepping forward over the baseline as you stroke; trying to muscle the racket head into the ball instead of letting the swing do some of the work, etc. Then practice your serve as CON-SISTENTLY as you can. Practice exactly the same serve for about a year until you have it GROOVED. Think "check-list" while you practice on EVERY service. Then once you have it grooved you can think more about how hard and where to hit it.

POWER IN SERVES

POWER can be developed after you have achieved a consistent serve. Consistent means that you can put thirty first serves in court out of a pail of forty balls, and thirty-five second serves out of forty. When you test your consistency, change from the deuce to advantage court every good service, just as in a match; that is, don't serve all forty balls from one position, since this does not simulate match conditions.

A large muscular man may use a simple, flat, overhand arm sweep with moderate wrist action. A medium-sized person may jerk his left shoulder down and bend forward from the waist; the torso thus snaps his right arm forward like a sling. Some bend their knees deeply, and as they strike the ball they straighten their legs; this shoves the torso up at the same instant they are throwing the racket head up and forward like a whip. The racket head, in some cases, seems to HESITATE a bit behind their left shoulder just before it is whipped up and forward. (Watch Roscoe Tanner's first serve.) Servers who rush the net after serve usually get a faster serve with less effort, because they really put their body weight into the forward motion of the serve and then keep right on driving to the net. The server who stays back will often stop his falling motion forward too soon so he can get into his defensive position on the baseline. This takes the sting out of his serve. So if you don't follow serve to the net, make certain to finish your follow-through completely before you take up your split stop on the baseline. A strong wrist snap at the end of your serve helps power also. Hitting the ball on the "sweet spot" (exact center of the strings) adds power. It is better to hit the ball between the center and the throat of the racket than to hit it between the center and the top of the frame. When you contact the ball way out at the end of the head it often feels dead or "boardy," probably because of less weight behind the ball and less leverage. In general, then, it might be better to overreach the ball than to underreach when you stroke, for more consistent power (but this doesn't mean to straighten your arm way out).

Well, anyhow, when the day comes that you can put thirty out of those forty first serves in court, start trying to add a little more power. In the main, try a little lower toss, a little farther out in front, a gradually increasing speed on the racket head, a little more bend in the knees on the start of service, plenty of weight transfer forward and UP, meeting the ball FLAT first, exaggerating your wrist snap forward and UP, plus a complete, stretched-out follow-through. And don't look DOWN as you drag that right shoulder through. That head position is more important during a hard service than in any other stroke. Don't slug the ball. A seven-eighths speed is enough. Always retain enough for control. Aim for that slit, not anywhere! Forget that score for at least six months until you gain consistency. Think about how you PLAY, not how you score, for a while.

Approximately 50 percent of all your strokes hit in a singles match, and about 60 percent in doubles, will be a service or return of service. Why not increase your concentration on these strokes? A serve is something you can always practice by yourself. Blast the balls into an old blanket on the clothesline, if nowhere else. You don't have a clothesline anymore? Well, hit them into your old gas dryer then.

SERVING IN DOUBLES

It is not necessary, or even recommended, to hit a hard first service in doubles. The faster you hit that first serve, the faster it comes back, and costs you approximately one or two steps toward the net, which means you end up with the ball landing at your feet instead of coming toward you about knee- or waist-high. (Obviously, if you are playing weaker opponents, and they cannot handle your first fast serve, then use it.)

Get the first serve IN. Statistics show that in doubles about 70 percent of first serves that go in, end in point for server. Only 50 percent of good second serves are won by server! This is assuming at least good intermediate-level serves. (Obviously a patty-cake slow serve would be a setup.)

Serve deep to the backhand corner most of the time. More serves to the forehand in the deuce court are suggested, since they pull the receiver way out of court and give the server's net man a chance to intercept the return. Stand AWAY from the center mark on the baseline for wider service angles.

If you DO follow service to the net in doubles, you must take several quick strides toward the open alley as you angle toward the net. Again it is a matter of bisecting the field left open between your partner at the net and the open alley opposite him. Again and again you see intermediates hit a good serve in doubles and then forget to cover the hole on their side of the court. They make the mistake of running directly toward the net instead of veering to the open side FIRST. And so the returns keep bounding away from them out the unprotected alley time and again.

If the server does not follow serve to net, he should still take several strides toward the open alley and come to a split stop, bisecting the field left open to the receiver's return.

Serve to Backhand corner

OVERHEAD

1. Watch ball, and if it is going to drop almost straight down within five or ten feet of the net, LET IT BOUNCE. It is much safer to hit a high, short lob after it has bounced. Your opponents are in position by this time anyhow, and it is much easier to time this setup ball than it is the one accelerating downward.

2. On a good lob, keep under the ball, and position yourself so its trajectory brings it down about twelve inches in front of your right eye.

3. Cock your racket back over your shoulder EARLY, with elbow high. (You do not have to go through the whole service windup, although some do.)

4. Point at the downcoming ball with your left hand until you start your stroke (see Illustration 1). This simulates your service toss position and tends to keep your left shoulder from dropping down before you stroke.

5. Skip into position, keeping your feet a little wider apart than usual, because it is more difficult to keep your balance with your head back.

6. Keep your left side toward the net and your right foot back.

7. From the cocked position stroke through the ball with an absolutely flat racket. Hit the ball on the "forehead," much as in the flat serve. You are usually forward of the baseline, and you don't need topspin.

8. Racket head should be in FRONT of hand at impact (see Diagram J). Don't overkill. The ball will come in plenty fast with a three-quarter-force stroke.

9. Watch the ball and then the point of racket contact a split second AFTER impact. Don't watch your opponents. Steady head is the key.

10. Aim for the large part of the court. For example, if you are on the right-hand alley, don't try a down-the-line

Illustration 1

impact

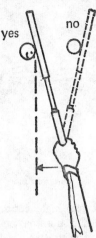

Diagram J

overhead. Aim for the center of the larger area to your left. This is no time to try for a hair-splitting placement.

11. Keep elbow high when cocking racket back over shoulder. Don't let the elbow get off to one side so that you make a swing with the arm bent at a right angle. (This can be done on some side shots, but with the regular overhead the higher you can contact the ball the better the chance to make a decisive smash.) The stroke should have enough wrist action and snap to give the shot power.

12. Keep pressure on the first two fingers of the right hand on impact.

13. The back of your hand should be facing the sky at the end of wrist snap.

If the ball is a sky-high lob let it bounce, even if it is in the backcourt. It will bounce straight up and will be much easier to time.

If the ball is sort of a poopy low one that has just evaded your racket and has dropped near the baseline to bounce

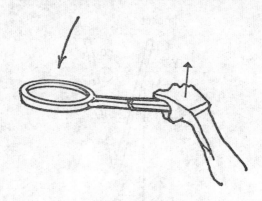

Diagram K

about seven or eight feet high, concentrate hard. You can usually get yourself into position on the left side of the bounce, and here you can use your right-angle arm stroke to play it as a slice serve. (It is too low usually to get under it for an overhead shot unless you were to get down on your knees, which some players literally do.) As you stroke, however, think "eighty-five feet." The court is seventy-eight feet long; you are usually running back; the slice is notorious for not giving your stroke any power; thus you need to hit it harder than you normally would. Practice a few dozen of these and you'll be surprised how handy that slice action is for control of those dink bounces that usually get hit into the bottom of the net. Remember, think "eighty-five feet," and hit with plenty of depth in mind.

FOREHAND DRIVE

You have probably already established the grip for your forehand somewhere between the two extremes shown below looking at the butt end of the racket. Some players change grips between forehand and backhand shots. Others use the same grip for both shots. Some advance the forefinger up the back of the handle a bit, others like the hammer grip where the tip of the forefinger meets or overlaps the tip of the thumb a bit.

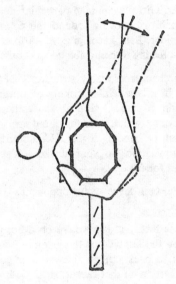

Diagram L

1. Pick your target area. Don't just hit it anywhere. Think TARGET before you stroke. Get in the habit of planning your attack one or two seconds before each stroke. Your drive is your best attacking weapon, but you limit its capabilities severely if you don't think about WHERE to place it as well as HOW to stroke it. (Someday try to

39

hit ALL your forehand drives into an eight-foot square in the opponent's backhand corner.)

2. Think DEEP. Get that drive into the backcourt no more than eight or nine feet from the opponent's baseline. (Watch where Rod Laver's drives bounce.)

3. Bend those knees, especially on low balls. The knees act as springs and load levelers, and allow you to adjust to variations in height and speed of incoming balls. Straight legs fix you to one rigid body position, which obviously has a high probability of NOT being the ideal position for meeting the ball. You do not have any starting traction, either. Girl players take particular note of this item. Get the habit of moving around the court like an agile crab or spider. Bent knees give you a look of aggressiveness and a feeling of being able to start quickly. Try it.

4. Keep your back reasonably straight. That is, don't bend way over in a bow while stroking or waiting for service. Your spine is like a vertical shaft that becomes the column around which your torso and arm rotate. Tipping it too much or bending it just adds another variable and more complications to your stroke. (Watch Ken Rosewall's erect torso.)

5. Watch the ball leave your opponent's racket. (Think target now.)

6. Move those feet. Act like you're on a hot plate. Get into position on the left side of the incoming ball FAST. You may have to back up, go sideways, or go forward, but get there early with that racket back. With weight coming off right foot step onto that left foot with bent left knee and then stroke.

   In some cases where your opponent is driving deep center balls most of the time you can simplify your footwork by stepping off with the right foot with a good stride and:

   a. If the ball comes at you, step toward the net with the left foot and stroke.

b. If the ball bounces farther away, step at an angle to the net and stroke.

c. If the ball bounces way out to the right, step the left foot and leg almost parallel with the net and stroke.

Thus two strides can cover almost any spot on the baseline against these deep center drives, if you add the length of your arm and racket.

Ordinarily you will be using a series of quick driving steps to get into position early. But whichever way you choose to move, always try to get that left foot across your body, out in front with knee bent, when you stroke that forehand.

7. Backswing EARLY. Watch the opponent's stroke as well as the ball coming off his racket. See if you can have your shoulder pivoted and your racket head well into the backswing BEFORE the ball crosses the net. Most intermediate players can improve their game immensely by getting the backswing completed early. Their commonest error (next to moving their heads before they have completed their strokes) is to wait until they are on the ball before they start their backswing.

You often hear players say of a pro, "He looks so relaxed and swings so easy. He doesn't seem tight and hurried, like I play." The reason for this contrast is partly that the pro has faster reflexes and a natural coordination that most of us do not have. But of much greater importance is the fact that the pro has practiced hour after hour on starting his backswing the INSTANT he can detect where the ball is going. If you can start your backswing even half a second sooner than you have been, you will be elated to find that you seem to have all the time in the world to stroke. Then you can really concentrate on leaning into it and aiming, instead of rocking back on your heels, barely getting the racket head around, and glancing the ball off the net post.

Another benefit from an early backswing is POWER. You may have seen a slight, fourteen-year-old girl blasting forehand drives down the line like a vet, and you think, "My gosh, she doesn't look that strong." Biceps are a very small part of continued power in tennis. Timing, body weight control, and racket head weight provide the punch. If you observe that little girl again, you will probably discover that her racket starts back early. Her backswing is often exaggerated, but it unwinds forward as she shifts her weight from the back foot to the front foot and continues with a long, smooth follow-through. She finishes with the racket head pointing way out toward the opponent's court, not wrapped around her neck. This long, smooth acceleration allows her to get optimum speed PLUS CONTROL out of the racket head. Thus she contacts the ball in the center of the strings at the correct angle just when the racket head is approaching its top speed. The weight of the racket head provides the force. Her arm then only has to provide the control. MEMORIZE "The arm is only necessary to provide the control." And it's thwack, thwack, thwack, time after time after time. BACKSWING EARLY and enjoy your tennis, instead of dabbing nervously and frustratingly at the last moment.

If the ball is coming fast, then shorten the backswing, but still try to get that backswing STARTED back early. The portion of your forward swing just before you contact the ball is normally about 30 percent of the total stroke. This first portion of your swing can be reduced to 20 percent or even 10 percent, as long as you have taken that racket head back early and started it forward in time to meet the ball AHEAD of your torso.

 8. Keep the backswing and forward stroke relatively level with the ground. Large, exaggerated backswing loopings complicate the swing and sometimes use too much precious time. If the ball is a low one, bend your knees more but keep the stroke level with wrist below racket head, even though it's only a foot off the ground. If the ball is a high bouncer, raise your shoulder and arm on the backswing and keep the stroke level even though it's six feet above the ground. This has an advantage, in that you are always using the same forehand stroke no matter

what level the ball and thus get more practice and more consistency. (See Illustrations 3, 4, and 5 under "Backhand Drive" for similar leveling.)

9. The racket and the hand rise gradually during the stroke forward. This provides the topspin upon impact as the strings pull upward on the back of the ball. (Try not to whip the racket HEAD upward in an exaggerated manner, since this means a short arc and little control.) The whole racket, hand, and arm gradually rise to meet the ball and keep right on going through it.

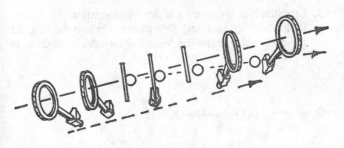

Court level

Diagram M

10. Don't let the racket head get below wrist. On low balls bend that left knee especially.

11. Keep the right elbow sort of tucked into the body during the backswing and approach to contact point. Then the arm is gradually allowed to extend as the racket impacts the ball, carries it, and follows through way out in front. This keeps the stroke a little more compact and helps with control. The racket head, in this case, is kept moving through the ball in more of a straight line (instead of an arc) as it contacts the ball and carries it along on the strings toward the aiming point.

NOTE: The arc made by a racket head swinging from a fixed point has only one point at which a ball can be sent to target. If you can change that arc to a straight

43

thrust, or at least to one of a longer radius, you have that much better chance of meeting the ball and carrying it on the face of the racket toward the target.

12. Some players keep the arm pretty well extended all during the stroke, locking the wrist and slightly flexed elbow. But they still keep the racket head and hand rising along the line of flight of the ball as above. The racket head is rarely brought up and around with a lot of wrist action on the follow-through, although this whiplike action adds a lot of topspin if you have the coordination to handle it.

13. Left shoulder is toward the net when starting the stroke. Right shoulder (see dot) follows the arm into the ball. At the end of the stroke the torso has turned so the chest is

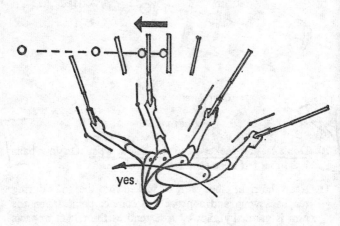

yes.

Diagram N

almost parallel with net, and you are ready for the next ball. Lean into the stroke, toward the net. Don't fall off to the left and let that right shoulder fall away from the stroke, as in the diagram below.

14. Keep your torso erect (watch Ken Rosewall) and feel as if you are rotating on your spinal axis. Don't get in an exaggerated bent-over position so that you feel your

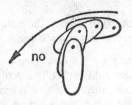

no

Diagram O

torso is swinging around a huge arc from the pelvis. This last just adds another variable and hinders consistency. Obviously when you have to stretch for a "way outer" you sometimes have to lean way over to increase your reach.

15. Aim for the drive to clear the net by a good margin. Place that imaginary aiming slit about two feet over the net if you are driving from midcourt, but place it about three or four feet above the net cord if you are driving from the baseline. Remember that the ball has to travel almost eighty feet when you are way back. If you aim too low, the topspin will carry the ball right down into the net instead of into the backcourt. Move that aiming slit UP as you hit from way back. Eighty feet is a long way for a ball to stay five feet above the ground all the way!

16. Contact the ball slightly ahead of your torso. This tends to give you better weight behind the stroke and better angular vision.

17. Keep eyes locked on contact point a split second AFTER impact. A steady head is the key to torso action. Don't peek up before or during impact like four million of your opponents do, and eight million golfers.

18. Keep your wrist locked, and SQUEEZE that grip to help it stay locked. Because you are contacting the ball slightly ahead of your torso, you have to bend your wrist slightly backward to insure that the racket face and handle are at a right angle to a line drawn through your aiming point when you impact. This is a good time to

45

remember Item 10 and keep the racquet head ABOVE your wrist a bit also as you lock it in position.

19. Hold grip firmly on impact. Don't relax grip as you stroke. A loosely held racket (particularly with women) accounts for more mishit balls than many players realize. It is the one bad habit that is almost impossible for even good coaches to detect. Many a ball twists the racket just enough to cause an out or a net. SQUEEZE.

20. Follow-through should end with racket handle as parallel with net as possible. Keep the right hand moving FORWARD as long as possible, and don't wrap your arm around your body, since this destroys all control in your follow-through.

21. Stroke moderately with more topspin from midcourt. From the baseline hit with less topspin and more power. Rather overdrive your opponents' baseline occasionally than give them a lot of short approach setups in their forecourt. THINK DEEP.

22. Keep those knees BENT on the forehand until the stroke is completed. Every time you straighten that left leg too soon (to get back into position) you not only lift your torso and angle of attack on the ball, but you also tend to stop the body weight from following through. The stiff left leg acts as a brace instead of a load leveler. (As your forehand drive becomes more consistent, it sometimes helps to "lift up" or straighten your legs slightly as you come through the ball. The added "lift" helps give a little more topspin.)

come to you
short & high

These are shots that you intend to follow up or approach the net immediately after stroking. They often occur when you anticipated correctly or your opponent erred and gave you a short, slow, high-bouncing return. Very often the intermediate player flubs it. He tends to whale away at the ball and knock it into left field. The reason so many of these setups are missed is that the ball is moving with less pace, and the player has more time to stroke than he realizes. Or he arrived in position much earlier than usual because of his anticipation. In either case he forgets to slow down his timing rhythm.

There is another factor here, an optical illusion, that intermediates do not understand. Let us say that a ball has bounced about nine feet back from the net and about five or six feet high (see Diagram P below). The player sees the whole court open from that position, and he gets the idea that all he has to do is slam the ball over the net and he has a thirty-by-thirty-foot target to hit. Now note in Diagram P that if he pounds the ball hard and its trajectory is almost flat, he will actually have to place that ball within a slit about one foot high slightly above the net cord in order to keep the ball in court. That's a pretty narrow funnel for an intermediate to slug a ball through, eh? Now, if he hits the ball moderately and follows through carefully, he has a slit three times wider through which he can still keep the ball in court! Which probability do you think the pro gambles on?

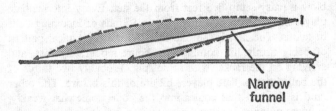

Narrow funnel

Diagram P

47

In general, then, coaches advocate the following on "easy" balls:

1. Take your time. Pick your target. Let the ball come to you. Don't swing too early. Wait!

2. Use a shorter backswing, but increase the speed of your stroke as you swing THROUGH the ball toward your target. Don't poke at the ball or flick it hurriedly with a wrist shot (short arc, no control). Actually, slow-bouncing balls are often HARDER to return than a ball with moderate pace and spin on it. You need to concentrate more, not less.

3. Contact the ball at the peak of its bounce. You get better angle.

4. Contact the ball ahead of your torso, as usual (just off the tip of your left toe on a forehand, for example).

5. Hit it moderately with plenty of follow-through for control. More often than not you are already coming in on the ball. You are moving forward, and a moderately controlled stroke plus your body motion and weight will give the shot plenty of speed. Get the ball in court and let the opponents make the error. If you slug it, you lose.

6. Keep eyes on contact point a split second after impact. How easy it is to "peek" on these shots and admire your beautiful "putaway" as it goes five feet out. "I should've had it" is the dreariest phrase in tennis.

Many times you see a player make a beautiful saving shot on the dead run from a far corner, but on the very next shot blow a patsy setup five feet from the net. Every intermediate player has to learn that there are two kinds of incoming balls in tennis. The first is the one that follows the typical pattern of being firmly hit, coming into court moderately fast, and arriving on the racket with some spin. Probably two-thirds of the balls intermediate players hit are of this nature. The other kind is the ball that comes into the court somewhat weakly, bounces without pace, and arrives on the racket with no spin.

More points are lost by intermediates on these so-called set-ups than on all the other "normal" shots put together. This is usually true because the rhythm or timing is interrupted, and the player isn't experienced or smart enough to slow down his timing, increase his concentration, shorten his backswing, get COMPACT, watch the contact point AFTER impact, and stroke MODERATELY through the ball.

Tennis games at the intermediate level are usually lost, they are not won. In other words, for every service ace or sharp placement for point there are about three errors or more made. The players who think checklist, use moderate strokes, and GET THE BALL IN end up with more points, because the opponents beat themselves by hitting too hard and forgetting control. When the ball is bouncing in your court you have THREE times the chance of making an error than of making a whiz of a placement. Think CONTROL now. Power tennis is of absolutely no use until you can stroke as unconsciously as you throw a stone. Groove that stroke first.

return to √ (1)

7. Another way to think of it is to hit the approach shot with control, say, to the deep backhand corner, and figure on making your putaway point on your NEXT shot from the net. And you will discover that 60 percent to 70 percent of the time your moderate first shot is unreturnable anyhow. What better statistics do you want?

8. Stroke to target. One of the simplest tactics to use for a short setup that landed on your right-hand alley near the service line is to return the ball "down the line" (that means to aim the ball so its path parallels the sideline). This will land it about two feet inside your opponent's sideline on his backhand as deep as you can. (2)

9. Bisect the angle from which your opponent will contact the ball (on his backhand) and move to a position slightly to the right of that bisecting line. Bisect the angle means that you estimate what line the opponent's return ball can follow to pass you on your extreme left, and what line it can follow to pass you on the extreme

49

right and then place yourself halfway between those two paths. By centering yourself in the field he can hit to, you give yourself the optimum possibility of getting to most balls he returns.

"O.K.," you say, "but why did you just tell me to move to a position slightly TO THE RIGHT of the bisecting line?" Well, observe closely now. If your opponent hits his backhand return "down the line," that is, past your forehand side, it has to travel about forty feet before it crosses the net. If he hits his return crosscourt, the ball has to travel about forty-five feet before it crosses the net. That means you have a little extra time to cut off his passing shot to your backhand. So by stationing yourself a little to the right (see position 2 in Diagram Q) of the bisecting line you are in the best defensive position.

10. Again, don't follow this advice blindly. You may discover that your opponent has a tough time hitting down-the-line shots off his backhand. Most of the time he hits a crosscourt chop from that position. Now, don't give yourself away by positioning yourself so far over to your left that it becomes obvious to your opponent. Instead, place yourself ON the bisect line with your knees bent. And just as he strokes the ball (his eyes will be on the ball at that moment and not on you), lift your racket high on the backhand, move at a slight angle toward the net as you move to your left, step across with your right foot, and punch it for a winner. The high racket head insures a downstroke; the motion toward the net insures the maximum chance of getting to the ball before it drops below the net cord and also adds a bit of force and body weight to your forward punch. A tactical maneuver of this anticipatory type will get you as many as six or eight points per set. And if you don't move until the opponent has his eyes glued on the impact point, he may never discover you are starting your short backswing even BEFORE he strokes. Pretty foxy, huh? Yes, he may occasionally get one down the line and fool you. But don't throw the whole tactical system out the window just because he

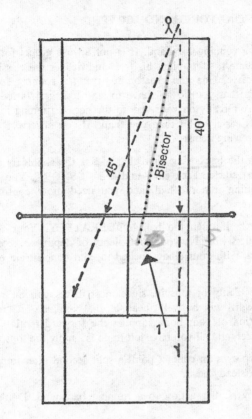

Diagram Q

made you look like a fool on one shot. Keep track of how many points you are getting off him. You can well afford one or two "goofs" and still smile all the way to the bank on the other six or eight points you made by taking that calculated risk.

RUNNING FOREHAND DRIVE

Learn a running forehand. It is not always gospel for an intermediate to stop, plant his feet, and deliver the classic forehand drive. One good reason for using a running forehand drive is that you do not have to stop and get started again. You are already on your way to the net. A running forehand drive is easier to hit than you think, if you observe a few of the following items:

1. Get the <u>backswing</u> (and that means the shoulders pivoted also) started back early and keep it SHORT. You will be running into the ball, and you need more control than power.

2. Stroke through the ball MODERATELY. Your forward motion will give your shot plenty of depth, so keep compact, with your <u>elbow tucked</u> in, and concentrate on control.

3. Use plenty of topspin, since most drives you hit running forward will be well ahead of the baseline. The forward motion of your body supplies the forward motion of the racket, and all you have left to do is supply the topspin.

4. Keep eyes on contact point a split second after impact for that steady head.

Apply similar action to a running backhand. Don't overhit!

Now, if you are way out of court and running SIDEWAYS a lot, you should not be worrying about how to stroke. You should be worrying about where you placed your previous shot! Because you probably placed it too high to a net man or too short to a baseliner. <u>Deep shots in the backcourt</u> prevent angled returns. <u>Low shots in the forecourt prevent speedy returns.</u>

52

FOREHAND CHOP

racket head + hand high

(See also "Chop" under "Return of Serve," Item 7.)

1. Backswing early.

2. Keep racket head and hand slightly higher than incoming ball as you backswing.

3. Use rather short backswing with slightly bent locked elbow.

4. Wrist locked. Don't flip racket head down across the flight of the ball.

5. Forward stroke is slightly downhill, but with racket movement primarily FORWARD. You must impart strong forward motion to the ball, and you cannot do this if the movement of your racket head is slicing downward excessively.

Illustration 2

6. Keep racket head slightly above wrist, and keep it that way through the entire stroke. Don't get the downhill action by snapping the wrist and dropping the racket head below the wrist.

7. <u>Racket face remains almost perpendicular to ground but with top of face tipped slightly backward</u> (open face), which sometimes increases as stroke nears completion.

8. Keep compact, with elbow close to torso for better control.

9. Step into the ball and toward net with that left foot. Keep left knee bent.

10. Let your right shoulder punch forward and do most of the work as it transmits the weight of your body through the locked bent elbow and locked wrist into the ball.

11. Meet the ball early, ahead of your torso. SQUEEZE.

12. Watch ball contact racket and keep eyes glued on contact point a split second AFTER impact.

13. Stroke THROUGH the ball. Don't bat it.

14. Hold handle of racket parallel to net as long as you can during follow-through.

   NOTE: Forehand chops tend to curve to the right, so when you hit a forehand chop down the right sideline allow two feet so the ball doesn't curve out.

BACKHAND DRIVE

1. Pick your target.

2. Start your backswing loop early and exaggerate that shoulder pivot. Use the left hand on the handle to help guide the head back, and then after you drop the racket below ball level, use the left hand to start the racket into the forward swing. This left hand is very necessary to give your stroke an early start.

3. Keep the right shoulder forward and LOWER than the left shoulder. This helps prevent the tendency to fall backward.

4. Pivot the left shoulder around so that your back is at about a forty-five degree angle with the net. Practically "turn your back" on the net. Let the back of your right shoulder "face" the ball.

5. Lean into the stroke, that is, toward the net.

6. Keep that right knee bent all the way through the stroke. There is a great tendency to straighten that knee and pull the racket across the body as the stroke is completed. (This panic stroke occurs because the backswing is started late, the ball gets too close to the torso, and the player FALLS backward, away from the ball, thus dragging the right shoulder along with the torso.)

7. Cock racket at an angle with the forearm on the backswing.

8. Lock your wrist.

9. As you swing, gradually straighten the elbow. The arm should be practically straight a few feet before you contact the ball (see illustrations below).

10. Keep the stroke relatively level with the ground but rising gradually through a contact point and follow-through, just as in the forehand drive. If the ball is high, keep your backswing loop high, with knees only slightly

flexed (see Illustration 3). If ball is low, make your back-swing loop low and bend your knees more (see Illustration 5).

11. Contact ball ahead of your torso.

12. Keep eyes locked on impact point.

13. <u>Keep racket head above wrist.</u>

14. Keep the WHOLE racket rising as you come through on the stroke. Meet the ball FLAT and let the strings pull up the back of the ball as you follow-through.

15. Keep elbow locked and wrist locked ALL THE WAY. (Do NOT break your wrist and flip the racket head over as you finish the follow-through.)

Illustration 3

Illustration 4

Illustration 5

16. The <u>angle</u> made by the racket <u>handle</u> and the <u>forearm</u> should be the <u>SAME</u> at the end of the follow-through as it was at the beginning of the stroke.

17. <u>Finish the follow-through with the hand high and the handle of the racket held PARALLEL with the net as</u> long as possible. (This insures again that, during the time the ball is nestled in the strings, the racket head is moving TOWARD the aiming point and not swinging out to one side.)

18. While you're trying to keep that racket head moving out toward your target, keep that right shoulder uncoiling forward. Don't let it pull across in front of your torso too much or this will pull the racket across the front of your body also and spoil your direction. In Diagram M under "Forehand Drive" you noted that the stroking shoulder was the back shoulder. In the backhand the stroking shoulder is the front one. This is why it is so important to get that front shoulder way back at the start of the stroke and then bring it forward during the stroke. If you START with the forward shoulder forward, it has no place to move during the stroke except sideways, which destroys control. So twist those shoulders early and uncoil as you stroke with the whole torso. Don't just use an arm flick, as most people do. (With average practice, six to eight hours per week, it will probably take a year to learn a good backhand. Because only a part of that practice time is spent hitting your backhand! That's why you need long-term goals in tennis IF you want to improve.)

If you feel you don't have enough strength in one hand, use a two-handed grip. Grab the handle snug above your right hand with the left hand. Some let the little finger of the left hand overlap the index finger of the right hand (sort of like a left-handed golfer). Let the right locked arm do the guiding and use the left hand to steady the racket head. Squeeze!

Illustration 6

If you're in the backcourt and get a high bounding ball to your backhand higher than your shoulder, don't try to keep your stroke level with the ground. Rather start the backswing at shoulder height and come UP on the ball. This will tend to give it some topspin and also start its trajectory slightly upward so it will carry deep into the opponent's court. A high backhand is a tough shot and one of the last to be learned. If you are playing someone who is better than you, try hitting everything you can on a high bounding loop to his backhand corner and you may be delighted to find that that is his one weakness. It is surprising how many fair players cannot handle a high backhand. Most intermediates try hitting this type of ball straight ahead or try to climb on top of it and hit down on it. Don't. It'll never reach the net.

Regarding backhand grips: Some like to run the thumb up the back of the handle. Others angle the thumb across the back of the handle. A few like the hammer grip, in which the thumb is wrapped straight across the handle to meet the tip of the index finger. Some keep their wrist flat (that is, the back of the hand and the top of the wrist make a flat plane). Some like to ADVANCE the wrist joint a bit on a down-the-line drive (or, in other words, lay the hand back), since this helps insure that the racket face stays fairly parallel with the net and also prevents the racket face from slanting back or "opening up" too much. (This is very similar to Item 18 under "Forehand Drive," when the hand is laid back a bit also.)

Remember that your wrist joint action is similar to a ball-and-socket action, not just a hinge action like the elbow. You can lock it all right, as the books tell you, but in which position do you lock it? If you have a reasonable backhand drive, leave it alone. If not, experiment a bit.

Let's say you have the typical backhanditis, which is usually caused by having the racket face too open (slanted back at the top). This causes the drives to fly way up in the air, so the weak player generally compensates by bending his elbow to turn the face downward. But now he has that unlocked flapping hinge action in the elbow, giving him a different angle every time he strokes. Result: one shot out of five going in, and no confidence. (Some players have a knack for using this very stroke, since they seem to be able to lock the bend in. However, if you're the type with no confidence and no points . . . why not try a change?)

Try placing the racket face perpendicular to the ground, grip the handle, and straighten the elbow. Now bring the racket into the backswing about shoulder height and let the elbow bend slightly. Drop the racket and right hand to about knee height and as you come forward into the stroke let the elbow straighten and lock again a foot or more just before contact. Keep the wrist firm. Now swing through a few slow swings and watch the racket face. Does it still slant back? Adjust your grip (not your elbow) a bit until you are able to

60

keep the face fairly perpendicular to the ground even through a few faster swings. (Don't drag that right shoulder across the front of your torso!) Keep the racket head slightly above the hand as you stroke. Keep that handle parallel to the net as long as possible.

Now start hitting a few balls. Drop them well out in front of you, step into them, and try driving them crosscourt at first. This usually insures that you hit the ball ahead of your torso. Try thirty balls with that grip, wrist lock, and straight elbow REGARDLESS OF WHERE THEY GO. If it seems to be working, great. Memorize your finger, wrist, and handle position. If the thirty balls all end in the net, adjust. If they end in the sky, adjust. But don't do any grip adjusting until you have tried at least thirty or more balls with a predetermined grip. What feels awkward to you at first may suddenly start to bring them in. Give the locked straight arm a chance and squeeze that grip. Anyone smart enough to play tennis is smart enough to analyze a stroke, but you must realize that it takes constant checking and an awareness of your own capabilities as well. (You can work this same procedure on all your strokes.)

Locked st. arm

BACKHAND CHOP

1. Pick your target point. A chop gives you maximum control. Thus you should pick a SQUARE FOOT to aim for, rather than a general area, as one tends to do with drives.

2. Start your backswing early, keeping the racket head higher than usual. In other words, start the forward stroke above the point of impact.

3. Racket path should be mainly forward and slightly downward.

4. Keep racket face almost perpendicular to ground, facing slightly upward. The forward-downward stroke and slant of face gives ball backspin.

5. Racket head remains above wrist all the way. (Don't snap the head of the racket downward across the line of flight of the ball!)

6. Wrist and elbow locked, just as in forehand drive. (Some use a bent elbow, but there is a great tendency to flail it around on the backhand stroke.)

7. Stroke should be compact, with NO wrist action at end of follow-through.

   NOTE: Backhand chops tend to curve to the left, so when you hit a backhand chop down the left sideline aim about two feet inside the line so the ball doesn't curve out.

The locked wrist and elbow suggestions are pretty standard procedure for most normal strokes, since they eliminate a lot of variable motions. However, every tennis player knows that on "abnormal" strokes (of which there are plenty in every set) the wrist and elbow become "savers" on many shots. When the ball gets too far out in front or way behind you, it is the last-moment wrist action that makes the shot by cocking the racket face at just the right angle to get the ball back. When the ball gets too close or too far out, it is the elbow that has to react, also to recoil or extend as you stroke. Thus these checklist suggestions are meant as suggestions to help limit, but not stifle action. Don't think of your arm as a rigid pipe, or worse, as a limp piece of rope. Think of the arm as a semiflexible cable ready to react but not overreact. O.K.?

RETURN OF SERVE

(See also "Twist Service," Item 7.)

1. Before your opponent serves, pick your target area and pick your stroke. Lob, drive, or chop? Standing just behind baseline for first serves and just inside baseline for second serves are basic positions to be modified as you discover the type of service and bounce coming at you.

2. Keep back straight. Don't hunch over too much.

3. Get ball on peak of bounce or on the rise if you can. Gives you a better angle for return and gets it back a bit quicker. If you're not getting your backswing started early, you will have to back off and hit the ball after it has started its downhill path.

4. Bend those knees. Many players take a hop just as the opponent's racket contacts the ball. As they come down off the hop (or in some cases merely rising on their toes) they bend their knees like a coiled spring and thus are ready to drive off to either side. It saves maybe a half second reaction time, since it starts the muscle pattern early.

5. Start watching the ball when the server throws it up and continue to watch it leave his racket. Don't just watch him serve. This gives you a slight advantage in anticipation also.

6. Start racket into your backswing BEFORE the ball crosses the net. On making the backswing make certain that you pivot your shoulders as you take the racket back. (Just swinging the arm back gives you no power.) In the case of a fast service that comes to your backhand most of the time, start your backswing just as he contacts the ball. If you wait until the server is looking up at the ball, he will probably never realize you are anticipating his serve and getting set for it. Yes, you may occasionally get fooled by one down your forehand, but

again, balance the points against the errors before you abandon the tactic.

7. Lean into the stroke. Don't fall backward just because the ball is coming fast. If necessary, back up a step before the serve comes and then step forward as you stroke. Stepping back or leaning back is the surest way to muff a fast serve. This means that your body weight is going with the ball and all that is left to repel the invader is the weight of your arm, which ain't much. You MUST move forward into the stroke, SQUEEZE harder to keep the racket from twisting, and keep your head STEADY whether you have intended to drive it, chop it, or lob it. Control the ball. Don't let it push you around.

Fast services can often be returned with more margin of safety with a chop. Keep your stroke slightly downhill but with main emphasis on the FORWARD motion. (See Illustration 2 under "Forehand Chop.") One problem in doubles with using a chop as a return is that it tends to be slower and keeps rising. Thus it is easier for the net man to poach. So it must be kept low and wide.

8. Meet the ball before it gets even with you. Better vision, more power.

9. Stroke THROUGH the ball. Don't increase the speed of the racket head at the last moment, and BAT the ball back. Keep the stroke fluid with gradually increasing speed and continue that force right on through the ball into the follow-through. Feel as if the ball is stuck on the strings a foot or so before it springs off the face of the racket.

In general, the return-of-service stroke, either chop or drive, is somewhat shorter and more COMPACT than the longer backswing feel of the other ground strokes. The backswing often tends to be shorter and the elbow often stays closer to the torso during the early part of the forward swing.

65

10. Keep racket head above wrist. This is mainly to help insure that you're getting that front knee bent and getting DOWN on the low ones. Helps wrist stay more solid also.

11. Hold handle parallel to net as long as possible during follow-through.

If server stays back in singles, aim your returns deep to his backhand corner within nine feet of his baseline. If he rushes the net, lob or make returns lower so they drop at his feet or at least get below the net cord before he reaches the ball.

If the server stays back in doubles, hit crosscourt toward the open alley. If he comes to the net, lob or send back low returns so he has to hit up. Keeping returns low to the incoming opponent forces him to hit upward and prevents him from getting too many high balls, which he will probably blast right back past you.

Lobs may not appear very effective as a return of serve early in a match, because the players are fresh, and they often put 'em away for an easy point. But if you never lob, the opponent only has to concentrate on one action: getting to the net. If you lob occasionally, there remains in his mind that alternative. Will he have to stop, back up, and wind up? Also, overheads still take a lot of energy and are usually the first stroke to go haywire when fatigue sets in. So balance the points you are losing now on some lobs against those points you are probably gaining by his not being able to tear for that net as fast as he would like. By mixing your shots you keep him guessing; and in the third set, three or four lobs in a row may find him hitting them into the backstop. Long-term thinking like this over the entire length of a match is often referred to as strategy, whereas the shorter ploys and anticipations are referred to as tactics.

Although most doubles teams always play the receiver's partner toward the net, some pros keep the receiver's partner BACK near the baseline against a strong FIRST serve. (He has a better chance of intercepting poach returns by the server's net man after a weak return of first serve.) Then just before the second serve he moves up to the regular net position. Actually this tactic could probably be used a lot more in intermediate tennis than it is. There is a lot of poaching by the server's net man in intermediate tennis because of the many poor returns of serve that are too high, too slow, or too near the net man. Thus it is rather foolish for the receiver's partner to automatically go up to the net position when there remains that big chance of the server's net man intercepting the very probable weak return of a good first serve. And there is no bigger, more beautiful hole to hit through for the poacher than the space between a receiver back on his heels and his partner at the net.

There is a bit of psychological knowledge you may find handy in getting that backswing started early, particularly on return of service. When people are tested regarding reaction time between seeing a signal and making a muscular response, it has been shown that the reaction time can be shortened under certain circumstances. One test is conducted as follows:

The person to be tested sits in a mockup of an automobile seat and is told to press down on the brake pedal as soon as he sees the red light go on. If he is told to concentrate on SEEING the red light and then press the pedal as fast as he can, it takes him about three-quarters of a second to move his foot from the floor and depress the pedal. However, if he is told to keep his eyes on the light but concentrate on MOVING his foot, it takes him only about a half second to depress the pedal after the red light goes on. There is something about the sympathetic or autonomic nervous system that can bypass the recognition or perception centers, shunt the sensation directly to the response motor nerves, and clip a fifth of a second or so off reaction time.

Now let's see if we can apply this to return of service. As you wait for the serve, forget about trying to observe which side of you the ball is coming to. Instead, squeeze the handle, get the racket out in front, but concentrate on STARTING your backswing. Keep your eyes on the ball being tossed up by the server, but keep your whole attention on STARTING the racket back. Don't try to anticipate the ball in this case. Don't worry about whether you are going to backswing on the forehand or backhand side. Forget all that. Just think BACKSWING. Your response system will start automatically and correctly about a fifth of a second earlier than if you think "Ball . . . coming . . . direction, left . . . therefore, backhand backswing." Leave the sensory garbage out and go the direct response route. Try it. It may help you gain as much as a half second on the return of serve backswing, and that is gold. Maybe that's what coaches are talking about when they tell some worry-wart players, "Stop thinking so much and just play!"

One last suggestion: With many intermediates one cannot always tell where the serve is coming, because the server himself hasn't that much control. But the advanced player often has enough control so that he gets it to your backhand corner almost every time. After a few games you may note that he RARELY attempts to hit one to your forehand. Once you know what to expect, how can you turn the knowledge into points? Well, you can anticipate physically as well as mentally. Start your backhand backswing BEFORE he finishes his serve, but don't let him see you do it. The serve is one shot where your opponent's eyes are going to have to be looking up. So just AFTER he looks up, start your backswing and footwork. If you are careful, he may never discover you are anticipating his serve. If he is smart he may begin to suspect and try a balk (that is, make a poor toss and catch it instead of serving) and then watch your action instead of going through with the serve. Aha, caught in the act! Now a few start coming in to your forehand also. So the cat-and-mouse game continues. When playing an opponent who is just about even with you, it may be smarter to save the physical anticipations for key points and not risk the chance of giving away this advantage by exploiting it all the time. Relate your TACTICS to your longer-term STRATEGY.

VOLLEY

1. Be AGGRESSIVE. Go forward after the ball. Don't fall back and wait for it.

Illustration 7

2. In ready position hold the racket out in front of you at a flex arm's length with the racket head about as high as your head. Contacting the ball away from your waist gives you better vision. Stay closer to the net than a typical pro position. Intermediates don't hit that deep and hard, and the closer to the net you are the better chance you have of dumping it back in their court. (Advanced players usually stand about ten feet away from the net when volleying but stay ready to pounce forward on weak high return.)

3. Keep racket head high. Try to stroke ball downward (if it gets below the net cord, of course, this is impossible). But in intermediate tennis a sudden leap toward the net will often help you contact the ball about a foot or more over the top of the net and get you that important

point. Stay alert for those slower returns. (Watch a good badminton player.)

4. Keep your grip firm. SQUEEZE.
The volley is usually a short punch with no follow-through:

a. It can be delivered by using a short wrist snap at the end of a straight arm.
b. It can be delivered like a boxer by keeping the arm slightly flexed and then suddenly jabbing or straightening the arm with a locked wrist or a short wrist snap.
c. It can be delivered by keeping the elbow bent, wrist locked, and throwing the right shoulder forward with the body weight behind it, carrying the locked forearm and racket forward.
d. It can be delivered by having the arm out to the side and bringing the racket forward and in toward the torso from right to left with a chop action.
e. It can be delivered by having the racket head out in front with straight arm and locked wrist and then driving forward with the legs, keeping the eyes level with the racket head.

All the above strokes or punches are used at one time or another by different players in different situations. They have many things in common, however:

a. The backswing is short, rarely behind the shoulder, primarily a torso twist.
b. The stroke is compact, with a minimum of action in the joints.
c. The ball is contacted AHEAD of the torso.
d. The body is leaning forward into the shot.
e. The stroke is short, six inches to two feet at most.
f. There is sometimes a short chop action with the wrist upon contact.
g. There is no follow-through.

5. Keep those knees bent. Keeping your eyes level with the ball, when it is reasonably possible, will help keep those knees bent. Don't bow over too much. Keep your

back straight, your butt down. If your head is upright you get better vision. When your head is bent forward too much you tend to watch incoming balls through your eyelashes or out of the corner of your eyes, which may not be the best triangulation or cone of vision to judge speed and angle of incoming balls.

6. Keep racket head moving toward net. The two worst faults in volleying by intermediates are to poke the racket sideways in front of the ball with no forward motion (so the ball merely knocks the racket head backward and dribbles to the ground) or to hit at the ball with an extreme downward slice (so the ball merely knocks the racket head backward and dribbles to the ground). You must keep the weight of the racket head moving toward the opponent's court. Then it doesn't matter whether you hit it with the edge of the racket or the handle, you will have started the ball back the way it came. And that is crucial when you are only a few feet from the net. Even the term "blocking" a ball still means a locked strong wrist and weight leaning INTO the racket.

7. Hit volleys above net cord deep or at feet of opponents. Short, hard volleys tend to bounce high, and unless angled sharply are not too effective. Drop shots (taking the force out of the ball by letting the racket head move back upon impact) that drop weakly over the net to die can be used if one is well into the forecourt and the opponent is well back. (Drop shots are rarely successful when tried from the backcourt and not effective on important points like game or set point, because the opponent is at top concentration and will go all out for any shot.)

8. On low volleys below net cord, bend knees and keep wrist low and locked. Take your time! Low volleys are generally slower because they come from a low shot and are arching over the net. Most intermediates hit wildly and too soon. Stroke EASY just to clear the net cord so ball drops immediately, forcing opponent to hit

71

up again. If opponent is ten or fifteen feet back, peak
the ball just over the net cord. If he is close to the net,
either peak on your side of the net so the ball is traveling downward as it goes over the net, or lob (see
diagram below). And here is one place a wrist sho—

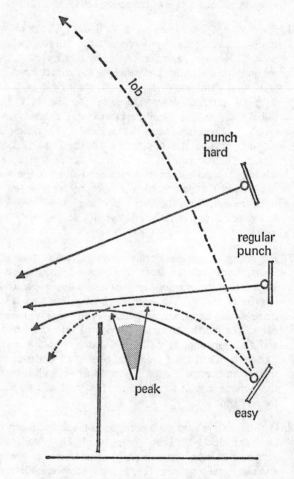

Diagram R

volley lob may be preferable to a locked-wrist, arm-stroke lob, because you gain a split-second surprise action at the last moment.

9. Lean into the volley. Don't get into the habit of falling back just as you hit. If you feel rushed, examine your other habits. Are you watching the opponent stroke? Is your arm way out in front, or is it back against your waist? Are you standing stiff-legged? Are you bringing the racket head back past your shoulder before you punch? This last habit can easily use up a half second, which means that the ball can travel ten to fifteen feet even on a slow shot. PUNCH or block, but don't flail away at a volley.

0. Watch the impact point! There is a greater tendency for players to peek or look up at the opponent on the volley than on any other stroke. The action is fast and there is little time to think, therefore it is important that the eyes tell the arm what to do ALL DURING the short punch and not look away during the crucial six-to-twelve-inch stroking area. Volley a hundred balls against a backboard two or three times a week for two months, and each time you punch say to yourself, "locked head." At the end of that time you will finally keep your head still and necessarily your eyes where they belong. You do not have to hit hard against the backboard, either. Just keep it easy and rhythmical. You really don't have to learn to volley. You have to learn to hold your head still.

1. Volleys require no follow-through. A volley is often answered with a volley, and there is no time to recover from a long follow-through action. So don't let the wrist flip the racket head around after the volley. Your arm will be almost in the ready position for the next shot to either side if you keep the punch short, compact, and locked.

Some players always use a backhand grip at the net, since is easier to hit a ball coming right at them with this grip. thers like the grip that allows them to hit either a backhand or a forehand volley (like the hammer grip), and they keep the racket head so far out in front of them that they rarely allow a ball to get closer than arm's length. Take your pick and then stick with it and remain consistent in your approach.

Many intermediate players never lob on return of service and cannot return a serve down the line, so their answer is ALWAYS the crosscourt return in doubles. If your partner is serving and you notice this while playing net on a first service in the deuce court, try the following: Shift your grip to your forehand punch grip; look over the net cord so you can see the service line; get your weight on your left leg; and if the serve is in, bring your racket back to shoulder, rather high, and start to the right but angle toward the net at the same time. Moving slightly toward the net gives your racket head a little more movement toward the opponent's court. One good stride with the right foot and a crossover with the left leg should put you just about in position to ram one down center between the opponents. Keep your elbow flexed. If the ball is a wide one, tough, let it go to your partner. Don't stretch way out with extended arm and racket and try to get it. You'll blow it every time BECAUSE YOUR RACKET HEAD IS NOT MOVING FORWARD and there is no weight behind it. Poach only if you keep that elbow flexed or wrist cocked. Imagine you have a shoestring tied between your cocked racket and shoulder, and if you break it, you lose. If you can reach the ball with a punch stroke you have it made; if not, forget it. On the advantage side use your backhand grip. This type of poach is recommended for use on first serves only, and don't overdo it. Poaching on second serves is rare unless the receiver is making weak returns, because the chances are against you. There is an old saying that you shouldn't poach unless you can put it away. Your doubles partner may remind you of this quaint saying after you have poached and the opponents still won the point. However, remember that tennis is a match, not a point or a single game. By poaching occasionally you make the receiver nervous. He tries to put his return a little farther toward the sideline, and thus his margin for error is that much greater.

74

2. One hears many players, particularly girls, say, "Oh, I'm a terrible net player!" and then back it up by cowering in the alley while their partner runs his head off chasing the incoming balls all over the court left wide open by his timid partner.

There is only one way to be a good net player and that is to be a TIGER. Let's say your partner is serving in the deuce court. Stand about eight feet back from the net (as a starter) and about two feet to the right of your alley. Grip your racket firmly (SQUEEZE) and hold it out in front of you at flex arm's length, even with your head. As the serve passes your shoulder start to move toward the center of the court at a slight angle toward the net, and make an effort to punch the opponent's return back. (If you keep that racket head in FRONT of you, you won't get hurt, which is the real reason many players hate the net.) Even if his return goes way crosscourt, make the EFFORT. Every now and then a return will come within your reach and you can get in your punch. Sure, you'll muff a lot, but if you look aggressive and act aggressive it makes the opponents nervous. Instinctively they'll try to keep it a little farther away from you. And occasionally you'll get suckered by having one go down your unprotected alley. But that'll only be one in ten or twenty balls. Forget it. Keep playing the percentages. Feint for the middle now and then and stay in the alley. Or stand listless-like in the alley and drive like hell for the center of the court as soon as the serve lands. Oh boy, what fun it is to take one like that. Again you don't have to overdo the theatrics, but do WORK. Plan, think, feint, watch that ball, and go for everything you can comfortably reach. That is the only way to play net. In no time at all you'll find you actually enjoy outwitting the receiver or at least making him apprehensive enough to flub a few. Attitude is 80 percent of the net game at the intermediate level. Be a TIGER.

And one word of advice to the partner of the beginning net player: LET THEM MAKE A FEW ERRORS! Encourage them to cover their half of the court. Don't start cautioning them about poaching. They'll learn soon enough about how far they can poach and how far they can't. They do need CONFIDENCE. When they ask you where to stand, tell them to stand wherever they feel comfortable. When they stretch like mad and sock one into the net, say, "Good girl, that's the way to go after them!" When they reach back for an overhead and the ball just ticks their racket and they look at you and say, "Guess I shouldn't have taken that one," you say, "Baloney, you take EVERY-THING you can reach. Prowl that net, Tiger, let's go!" Give your net player encouragement and backing. And believe you me, inside of five or six sets you'll have a partner you never knew existed.

HALF VOLLEY

1. Get low, if you have time, with right hand almost grazing the deck. If the ball is at your ankles let the racket hang straight down, but keep your hand forward of the racket face.

2. The top side of the racket face is kept forward (closed face) to sort of trap the ball just as it leaves the ground (see diagram below).

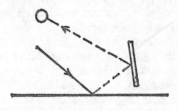

Diagram S

3. Watch the ball until you complete the contact! This is very difficult to do for the intermediate, because a ball even with his feet means usually that he is out of position and probably scrambling to move out of the way. He is very apt to look at everything except the ball near his ankles. (Pros often expect half volleys, especially on the way to the net after service, and they are able to anticipate and keep themselves off to one side in the optimum position.) Half volleys are much easier to handle than they look, if you can force yourself to look DOWN at that ball, even though you may feel it is going to bounce up and smack you in the nose. Your arm will do the right thing if you let your radar system give it the right instructions. But how can your arm stroke the ball correctly when your radar system is scanning the net post or the sneer on your opponent's face?

4. Short follow-through. More like a blocking action.

GETTING TO THE NET

As you become better and start playing stronger opponents you will find it is difficult to get up to the net position in one move. The balls seem to come back faster from the receiver and end up near your knees or feet when you are only two or three steps in from the baseline. Now you can stay back as a baseliner, wait for a good approach shot, and then go for the net. But it is better for most active players to accept the fact that you are only going to get about halfway to your best net position on that first ball. Come to a split stop as your opponent strokes, make the best shot you can from "no man's land," and then take two more steps in to your "best" position. Make that low half volley or volley carefully. Get it deep if you can or low if the opponent is rushing in. Make him hit from way back (gives you more time to get set) or from below the net cord (ball comes back slower). Don't try for a winner by shooting for a corner, since you usually don't have that kind of control over half volleys and low volleys. Just get it back and think of two variations of his return:

1. The opponent has anticipated and is well balanced, ready to try a passing shot.

2. He has not anticipated and is off balance, back on his heels, or struggling to reach your return.

In case 1, take your remaining two or three steps in to your net position, since this gives you a better chance to cut off his angle of return.

In case 2, move forward only slightly, because he may very likely throw up a lob, which will put you in good position to handle it. Or if he does try a passing shot, it will probably be weak enough so you can step in and get it in time anyhow.

1. Watch his racket contact the ball.

2. Come to a split stop. (Watch the ball coming.)

3. Be aggressive. Lean toward the ball. Attack. Don't fall back.

4. Keep knees well bent. (Watch the ball coming down toward your racket.)

5. Wrist low and locked. (See if you can read the trademark on the ball.)

6. Head locked with eyes glued on the ball until it contacts your racket face. There's plenty of time to look up AFTER the ball starts back.

7. Keep your knees bent throughout the stroke. Don't straighten up.

8. Advance to split stop.

LOB

Remember, on a lob it is a shorter distance from the peak of the trajectory to the bounce than it is from the contact point to peak (see diagrams below).

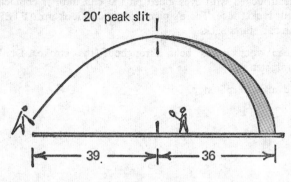

Diagram T

Roughly, then, the peak of your ball's flight should be about half the distance between you and the opponent's baseline. (This gives you a two-to-eight-foot allowance for the ball to land inside the opponent's baseline.) If you are near or behind your baseline when you stroke, use the net as reference and think PEAK over the net. If you are in the forecourt, think PEAK over a line halfway between the net and the opponent's service line.

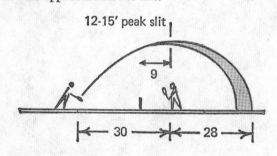

Diagram U

Instead of picking an area on the opponent's court for a target, move that aiming slit (the one we used for serves and ground strokes) up to twenty feet or so, and use that as your target as you stroke. Think PEAK and shove the ball up through the slit so the ball starts its downhill trajectory just after it passes through the slit.

1. At baseline think twenty-foot-high slit and PEAK through it.

2. In forecourt think fifteen-foot-high slit and PEAK through it.

3. Watch ball contact racket face.

4. On slow balls get under the ball and push the ball up with usual locked wrist, locked elbow, and flat racket. Don't flick at it. Get your shoulder and arm into the stroke and S-H-O-V-E it up to the slit. (Pros sometimes add topspin to a lob so that it bounces away from the opponent, but forget that for now and stick to the flat PUSH stroke for better control.)

5. On fast balls a combination blocking action and short chop stroke with very little follow-through is often used. It needs a locked wrist and a touch that comes only after about a year's practice. In the forecourt particularly, the racket head is sometimes allowed to drop BACK after contact with a fast ball (as in a drop shot) but with enough force left to pop the ball over the net man's head.

If the wind is blowing in your face, peak the ball farther toward your opponent's baseline. If the wind is behind you, peak the ball closer to you. It is said to be easier to lob into the wind than with it, but if you think PEAK with the wind in mind, you should be able to use a lob anytime. If the wind is blowing strongly from, say, your right side, aim your lob to fall outside their sideline on your right and then watch the wind bring it in. This sideways-bouncing ball is one of the craziest things to hit because it is very rare that players ever have to hit a ball traveling parallel with the net. You may not like to play in the wind, but remember that tournaments are rarely stopped because of wind. Wind can be as much of a challenge as a hard service. Learn to react under all conditions, and you will have more confidence and be less likely to give up or panic under tournament conditions.

Professionals refer to lobs as defensive or offensive. Defensive is generally the high lob hit when you are back on your heels or way out of court and struggling just to get the ball back so you can scramble into position. Offensive is the planned low lob just over the net man's head, often hit as a surprise tactic in the forecourt off a short bounce or a volley. However, in "C" tournaments or intermediate matches the lob can become an offensive weapon regardless of where it is hit from. It can be used, for example, even though your opponent never leaves the baseline. A lob for an intermediate player is often one of the worst dilemmas. Should you wait until it comes down and then drive it? Should you let it bounce and then reach up and slice it? Should you really try your overhead before it hits the ground? I have heard many players grumbling to others, "Don't play with that guy. All he does is lob you to death. It'll ruin your game!" Actually a player who lobs a lot should be sought out. So he beats you. In the meantime, start practicing your overheads. What a chance! Let him do his "worst" and cock your racket, elbow high, point at the ball, keep the racket face ahead of your hand at impact, hit it flat, and pound them three-quarter speed day after day. You'll get other balls too, and you will probably find he doesn't lob as much as they said he does. If he's winning, he is a better tennis player than you are, which means he is tenniswise and merely uses the old bromide, "Never give 'em a ball they like." If you think about it, the person who is really "ruining your game" is the player who always drives everything crosscourt to your favorite forehand. Boy, those rallies you get. "Why, that ball went back and forth fifteen times the last point. That's really tennis!" It is? Does it win for you? What you really meant to say was, "That's really rallying!"

Oft-quoted lines: "I know I believe I understand what I think I said, but I am not certain I realize what I said is not

82

what I meant." Which in tennis jargon means, "Players with all-around games never grumble."

A crosscourt lob gives you an extra length of court for safety.

A lob over the backhand side of the opponent is harder for him to handle.

Some points call for certain tactics. If you're ahead 40–0, you may want to risk five cannonball services in a row. If one goes in, it may mean an ace or a weak return. If you're behind 15–30, pick his weakness area and make your return steady. Get that deuce count. The score of 15–40 is bad odds to win a game. By working harder on these critical points, you will, in the long run, have a better game.

The first point of every game and the first game of every set are very important. It is the time when players are not concentrating quite as hard. Especially the player who has just won a close set very often tends to relax. This is the time to break his serve. Concentrate and play his weaknesses now.

Call the score before each service during a match and insist that the opponents do the same. There is nothing more irritating than losing a game because your opponent forgot to give you that second-last point. If the server does not call the score before he serves, it is perfectly correct to hold up your hand and request the score. This may annoy some players who never call out the score, but that is their problem, and they are usually the first to complain when their opponents get confused regarding the score. In friendly sets it is not that critical, and particularly deuce and ad calls are often sloughed over once deuce is reached.

Put it where they ain't. Or as one veteran player says, "Jerk 'em around the court." I was watching a tennis clinic in Pasadena on a Saturday morning about six years ago. One of the top professional players in the country was playing each of the advanced players for about five minutes. He would then give them his opinion of what their greatest weaknesses were. As he rallied with them he would start off with drives and then suddenly he would chop to the deep corners, slice to their sidelines, topspin to the other sideline, drop shot over the net, throw up a lob, etc. It was sort of horrible to watch, because the majority of the students, who were rather good high school or college freshman players, were sliding, scrambling, missing, gasping for breath after maybe only a minute or so. It was the rare player who could even return three in a row. Then the old master would say, "You know, if you're going to play tennis you just HAVE to learn to move. And you can't use a drive for every shot." Then he would show them how their footwork needed simplifying, how they were still running when he was stroking (they should be at a split stop), how they gave away their own shots, etc. Obviously they had heard this all a hundred times before, but it never dawned on them until that morning what a chasm existed between themselves and a professional player. At the end of the morning each one of those student players was a little bit humbler and was listening with wide-open eyes and ears cocked forward to catch every word.

The point to be gained here is that too many intermediate players only have one or two reliable strokes. They learn to play a certain type of crosscourt driving game, which is popular, because one usually learns the forehand drive first and then stops learning. Just try this one suggestion. Spend a summer learning a good fast-moving forehand chop. The next year when you are playing one of your forehand driving buddies, start returning a mixture of drives and chops. The chops have to be as deep as your drives to make the test fair, but you will probably find he will hit the chops way out or in the net just because he has always expected a ball with forward spin, in the backcourt, bouncing four feet high.

Tired at the end of a second set? Don't let the opponent know it during a match or a tournament. Sitting with your head between your knees and sighing big gasps won't help you recover any faster, but it does let your opponent know you're beat. Don't worry, he's darn pooped too. Instead, walk briskly to the sideline, towel off, take as long a breather as you can, and try to get back out on the court before the opponent does. Try a few practice swings, as if you're really ready to go again. No need to overdo it, but tennis is part poker as much as it is part chess. Tiredness is relative. If he thinks you're feeling peppy, it'll make him feel that much more like a sack of mush. Hide your fatigue.

Mental grousing about bad calls will lose you two or three points before you know it. Mental bitching interrupts your concentration on the next ball. Be a man, not a baby.

I think if you have ever visited a veterans' hospital and seen how cheerful and selfless some of those terribly wounded men are, and what they would give to be in your shoes, playing out in the sunshine, exercising to their heart's content, you would realize what a trifling thing a bad call is. Count your blessings. Be more aware of the beauty of the game. Sock that ball, have fun, and stop thinking in reverse.

Get the tournament attitude. Bad calls, bad weather, being behind, a cut finger, a cocky opponent can all be irritants. If you let these minor things bother you, you'll play your least effective game. Think of it this way: I may not have won this game, but I AM going to win the next one, because I am going to hit all the balls to his deep backhand corner where he is the weakest. I lost that first set, but I am going to get the first three games in the second set, because he has a hard time with low balls around his feet and I am going to chop him silly for three games win or lose, etc. In other words, HAVE A PLAN. Even if you are losing the match, play hard and go for everything. If you lose this match, there's always another tournament next month. If you are losing with your standard game, change it. Go for broke. Hit your strokes with confidence. You can at least "look good" as you bow out instead of chickening out with timid dabs.

In the spring of 1970 a friend and I entered a "C" tournament of sixty-four doubles teams. We got through the first round. That left thirty-two teams. Our next opponents defaulted, never showed. That left sixteen teams. We won the next match in three sets, and there we were with the last eight teams. Our next opponents were much stronger than we were. Faster drives, good crisp net volleys, and one of them had a high-bounding topspin twist service that we never got near breaking, let alone returning. They took the first set 6–2 almost without breathing hard. We couldn't see anything to even plan around. It looked like a dismal afternoon.

There was one small thing we did notice near the end of the first set. One of them was hitting slower overheads. Not weak, mind you, just a little slower than his fast-smashing partner. It was all we had, though. So every shot we could we lobbed over this player's head. They took the first two games, but then he started to miss. We took the next three. They had a conference. The next time we lobbed, the good player ran behind his partner, took the ball, and returned it. Sometimes he would get it early enough for an overhead, sometimes he would take it on the bounce. They took the next game. Three-all. We took two. They took two. We took one. They took one. Six-all. The tournament required sudden death (best of nine points) at six-all. Now, I suppose the happy ending would be that we won. We didn't. They took the sudden death, 5–2. And they deserved it. If we had won, it would have been a fluke.

But the moral is, forget the stuff going against you. PLAN and play like mad for the NEXT point, the NEXT game, the NEXT tournament. When we shook hands, the better player said, "Man, you had me scared stiff! I thought we had it made after the first set." Later we found he got as far as the quarter finals in the singles part of the tournament. Anyhow, we had a great match and had collected about thirty people watching that one set. I don't believe there has ever been a set in Southern California that consisted of all lobs and all overheads. We sure learned a lot about getting overheads back by blocking them on the rise and letting the topspin carry them back into another lob. The other partner said, "I'm telling you, if I had to hit one more overhead, my arm would drop off." Then we all laughed and clapped each other on the shoulders. Man, what a game it can be when you use your head and don't just fizzle out. Oh yes, the combined ages of our two opponents was ten years less than either of ours.

Keep your cool. There is nothing more apt to lose you points than losing your temper. Getting angry tends to destroy most of your concentration. In 1938, a friend of mine, Jack, and I entered a tournament in one of the states near the Great Lakes. It was for players from the southern part of the state, and the seeded No. 1 team was from the state capital. One of the players of that team was the public courts singles champ from the capital city. The matches were to be played on clay courts, but the tournament was plagued by gusty winds and intermittent showers.

Actually this was a godsend for us. Jack and I had played on homemade clay courts in a small rural town most of our lives. There were two lonesome public courts in our town built on a rise overlooking a gravel pit. And if there was any wind off the prairie at all, you can bet your sweet patootie it whipped out of that gravel pit and swirled around those courts like a dervish. The town did not maintain the courts, so we kids did the weeding, sewed up the net, drove out to the river to dig clay to fill up the winter frost boils, and in general, had a ball. There were only a handful of people who played tennis in town, and those were mostly kids. We probably spent more time digging out rocks, rolling the courts, repairing torn canvas tape lines, or rolling out white lime than most city court maintenance men. We learned to play on certain parts of the court only. If the back corner of the baseline was wet and soggy, we would roll a chalk line around it and declare it out of bounds. Sometimes we would play with as many as two or three spots outlined on the court. Thus we could play sooner after a spring rain and not dig up our precious court too much. Then a day later these sump holes would be dried out, and we could play the whole court again. Well, anyhow, as we grew up, coaching each other out of books, we not only learned to place our shots in the good parts of the court, we also learned to hit to the lousy parts of the court where the clay was the thinnest and the base rocks stuck out a little, or to drop shot into that sandy place in the advantage court. In the summer we would pitch our pup tents out by the courts with scads of mosquito netting swathed around the tents, so we could get up at 5:00 A.M. and get in three sets before we had to report home for breakfast. Ah wilderness, those days are gone forever, but they sure helped Jack and me wade through that tournament.

The winds made us feel as if we were right at home on the old gravel pit. Shortly after a thunder shower we would look over the court and watch the puddling. When it was dry enough to play on we would walk over it and test the surface, feeling for soft areas, and we soon got to know those campus courts as if they were our own. Between the winds and the chops to the soft spots we somehow got through to the quarter finals Saturday afternoon. Our opponents were the seeded team, No. 1 who were supposed to take the cup.

We had a plan. Play everything we could to the champ's partner. His partner was not as good as he was, and for the moment that was all we had to go on. We lost the first set, 4–6, but near the end of the first set, C, the champ, started barking commands at his partner. Now, a few good directions from the top member of a doubles team is accepted operating procedure. But the closer we pressed them for points the more the directions became commands, and then snarls, like, "Get back there. Move! Couldn't you see that coming?" etc. His partner was an easy-going guy who was working his head off.

We went into the second set and kept holding our serves until 6–6, and as the action kept getting harder and tighter, C started poaching a little more and a little more. It was his partner's serve going into the thirteenth game, and during the short interval between games Jack and I agreed we would go for broke and drive the next six returns either down the line or right at C. Now, C had been having to stretch for balls for twenty-two games, with many of the shots being low chops. If he wanted to get in the game he had had to start fast for a poach at the net, or elbow his partner out of the way to hog a shot in the center court. Luck was with us. His partner double faulted to Jack the first point, and C turned, looked at him, and stood shaking his head. First service to me was long. Second serve I got set as if to put across the normal crosscourt shot, but instead I walloped a hard topspin drive right at C. He muffed it: 0–30. Jack drove his first return right down the alley. C had already started his drift across to poach, and it caught him going the wrong way: 0–40. Someone in the gallery giggled. Bless her little heart. C turned and heaved his racket against the backstop. While he was recovering it, Jack and I discussed whether we should return to our regular tactics or keep firing them at C.

Considering we were pretty hot, we figured we'd keep on pounding them at C. If we could make him think we had his number we'd take the third set too. If we slowed down now, even if we did take this set, they would sure as hell pick us off in the third. O.K. Next serve to me. I drove it right at C. He blocked it this time, but Jack lobbed it back. His partner got the overhead in and took the point. Nevertheless, C did not make a sharp volley, and he knew it: 15–40. Service to Jack, who walloped another one right at C. C got his racket on it, but it hit the wood and caromed off into limbo. Games 7–6. We took the next game on our serve: 8–6. Early in the third set, after taking another snide remark, C's partner said something to him, and from then on there was dead silence from C. We won the third set, 6–2, breaking C's service once and his partner's once. That earned us two nice little bronze medals. We got beat Sunday morning in the semis (trouble was, eh eh, that the courts finally dried out and got hard on us), but, boy, did we have our moment!

If C had complimented his partner occasionally and worked out a system of having his partner hit crosscourt returns in front of C so that C could poach slightly and bisect a wide angle of return, or something like that, I'm certain they would have taken us. As it was, their best player lost the match for them by having no plan, being arrogant, ill-mannered, and finally losing his temper.

C's partner played poorly in the third set also. There is always a certain security when you have a good partner and you are ahead. But your REAL TENNIS GAME is no better than the game you play when your partner is crumbling, or you are falling behind.

Didn't someone say once, "Character is how a person acts during adversity; not how he acts when things are going fine"? Grit your teeth and dig!

For the sick, the puny, and the halt: Most tennis is built on the idea of winning the match, as it should be. Previous paragraphs on "get the tournament attitude" are pretty typical of this approach. However, there is another meaning to the word "winning"—that of winning by just being able to get out on the court and play. Those of us with torn knee cartilages, slipped discs, weak heart valves, arthritic wrists, and coronary ischemia or dimming eyesight have to apply the longer-term approach of a more relaxed attitude.

We are still tennis idiots, or we wouldn't be out there with our knee braces, waist girdles, gasping breath, tape holding up a Bell's Palsy drooping eyelid, quarter-inch-thick lenses, and neck casts. We play as hard as we dare. We make certain there are no leaves, seeds, or sand lying around either. One bad slip may mean four weeks in traction and then two weeks hobbling about the court in a leg cast. In the back of our minds are the doctor's words, "Well, I wouldn't recommend 'spurt' sports, like tennis singles, for a man of your age" while we go tearing back under a lob. So we ease up a bit and conserve enough so we can stagger out again the day after tomorrow.

Young people can get by with a ten-minute warmup and play a pretty normal game. When you get around forty-five, you'd better warm up at least fifteen to twenty minutes or you'll lose the first four games of a tournament match against youngsters before you get your tennis legs. Hit ground strokes first for five minutes and then work into easy serves and gradually harder serves, with a few minutes of overheads at the end. My partner and I often go to an empty public court and play six or seven games of singles before we report for a tournament match. At fifty-five we have found that our problem in doubles is not endurance as much as it is getting going in the first set.

Rallying a short time is fine for warmup, but for most intermediates it is a waste of time as far as improving his game goes. In general, the rallier hits his habit shots without thinking, and strokes them TO the other player. If the ball comes in short he usually waits for the second bounce, since he is too lazy to anticipate, be on his toes, and scramble. If it goes wide, he lets it go and hits the other ball in his hand. In other words, he is doing all the things you should NOT do when playing a match. So each day, for fifteen minutes before playing, he reinforces all the bad habits he has.

Instead, have a program for rallying. Agree ahead of time with the other player that you would like to hit as many backhands as possible for five minutes, and what stroke would he want? During that time try to outfox the other player JUST AS IF YOU WERE PLAYING A

GAME. He, for example, will give you as many shots as he can to your backhand side of the court but would mix them up. Deep corner, short wide, high bounding, etc. You would do the same with the stroke he wanted. It's even fun to keep score, like one point for each error you make, and lowest score after five minutes wins. Then try a different set of strokes.

This type of rallying really helps improve your game, because you get INTENSIVE practice by using your check-list and analyzing each stroke. You are fairly certain each ball is going to be a backhand, so you have consistency in practice, but you must also return to split stop at center to be ready for balls that the opponent doesn't always get to your backhand side. This simulates game play, makes you think intensely, and also forces you to hit to the TARGET the opponent has asked for. This is the ONLY way rallying will ever improve your other strokes. Think about it and try it.

If you are older and have tried and tried your serve over a long period and you find that your topspin just isn't enough to bring your service into the court, here is a heretical suggestion. Stand back two or three feet from the baseline and serve from there. The extra few feet are usually enough so that your serve will drop just inside the service line. Now, this is usually frowned upon, because it takes the server longer to get to the net, and the ball is in the air for a longer distance and can thus be anticipated by the receiver. However, it is not the distance through the air that de-termines how easily a ball can be anticipated. It is the TIME it is in the air that is critical. Thus if you can hit a fairly fast serve that has only a mild drop at the end, it is better to use that from three feet farther back than to have to slow your service down from the baseline in order to get it in. And furthermore, if you are a little wheezy and don't make a big deal about charging the net anymore, this serve leaves you in just the right position for a baseline game. So who cares? I watched a rather frail lady in her sixties up at Santa Barbara use that idea. Her serves were landing almost consistently one foot from the service line in the backhand corner. She knew exactly how hard to hit for that distance. There is a kind of "I didn't know it shouldn't be done that way, so I did it" creativity in intermediate and public courts tennis. If it works, use it. If somebody can show you a better way, fine, but if that somebody just tells you that you shouldn't do it that way, beware. That sideways underhand slice may be one of your best weapons. Hang onto it and work it to death. But also, if it's not getting the ball back, have the sense to change.

Get blisters on your feet? Wear cotton socks under your wool socks. Any slipping will occur between the two sock layers instead of between your foot and the wool sock. When your socks get thin on the heel don't use them for tennis. If you do, then accept your blisters. If you must play with a blister or torn callus try two cotton socks under one wool and lace the shoe up tight. The less the foot slides inside the shoe the longer you'll last.

Trouble seeing? Get your prescription ground into dark glasses set in the wrap-around Air Force type of glasses with the long brass ear wires that curl around the entire ear. The frames are thin and don't mask your peripheral vision. They don't shake off and are a boon in bright sunlight.

Keep losing your racket? Those of us with arthritic wrist and fingers know how easy it is to suddenly lose control when the hand gets bent into a certain position. To save a number of cracked frames, screw a small screw eye into the center of the base of the handle. Tie a heavy shoelace to it and make a nonslip loop (like a bowline) in the other end to fit loosely around your right wrist. This does not interfere with your stroke, but it certainly rescues the racket from cracking up on the concrete every now and then.

Weak grip or slippery palms? Powdered rosin or a tennis glove may help. The gloves are made with or without fingers and have several different surfaces in the palm: soft leather, little rubber bumps like coral, or a chemical semi-sticky adhesive. The adhesive-like material is not very useful to those players who change their grip from one stroke to another, but may be very helpful to those who use a hammer grip on every shot. The adhesive takes a little extra time to pry loose to shift from backhand to forehand, for example.

A steady nonslip grip is worth at least four to five points per set.

As you develop that fast wrist snap in your serve you may discover that the racket tends to slip out of your grasp at the end of the snap. There is a tendency among intermediates then to not snap quite as hard so they don't lose their grip. Instead, try taping a big ridge about half an inch high around the base of your handle using half-inch-wide Duct-Tape (used to tape hot air duct joints together) or some other kind of tough industrial mastic adhesive tape. Then cover it with ordinary white adhesive tape to give it a rougher surface. The heel of your hand then lies against this ridge, and you can get more wrist snap with less danger of the fingers losing their grip. Even pros do this, because they feel they can get an extra few inches of wrist snap if they don't have to rely on only their fingers to hang onto the racket.

Got tennis elbow? So bad you can hardly hold a comb? You've even considered playing left-handed? Try a flexible racket, say after a month's rest of your elbow. The very flexible rackets seem to absorb the shock or vibration of impact and keep the worst of the shock from passing through your forearm into your muscle tendons. There is an article by Gene Nash in *World Tennis* magazine of September 1972, page 80, entitled, "How Flexible Is Your Metal Racket?" It compares metal as well as wood rackets in regard to handle, throat, and head flexibility. It might help to look this article over and choose as flexible a racket as possible within your game style. At least it worked for me. My elbow was so sore a few years ago I cringed every time I hit a forehand. In the last stages I ended up playing entire games with only a backhand chop, because that was the only stroke that didn't feel as if someone were driving a red-hot spike into my elbow. I switched to a very flexible steel racket, and although it took me several months to get used to it, I have had no trouble with the elbow since.

Gut comes in various gauges, from light to heavy. Hard-hitting pros seem to prefer the lighter strings, strung very tight, say, sixty to sixty-five pounds. This combination apparently gives a very taut hard surface with little give, and the ball comes off fast. Players who don't hit that hard, often use the medium-gauge strung to about fifty-five or sixty pounds. This combination gives a little more resiliency; the ball sinks into the strings a bit more, and supposedly the player has a bit more control. "Soft"-hitting players, or those who use more spin or chop, often prefer less tension on their heads also. Many intermediates use the nylon or other synthetic strings because they are cheaper, aren't as subject to moisture changes, and thus last longer. Tensions from fifty pounds on the nylon up to fifty-seven or fifty-eight pounds are about the usual range for most Saturday players. Stringers tell me that tensions beyond fifty-eight pounds on the synthetic strings don't have much effect (that is, the extra tension doesn't give you anymore power, it just shortens the life of the strings and makes the face "boardy"). One stringer told me that synthetic strings also tend to stretch more than gut after a period of use and lose their original poundage. Evidently the gut is still the optimum stringing material for professionals and has more recovery (or whatever the scientific term is) at high tensions than the nylon. I used to ask for nylon strung at fifty-four pounds. Since writing this book I find my strokes are harder with a bit more control, so the last string job I ordered was gut at fifty-seven pounds. It's probably psychological, but I think it makes my serves come in harder with less effort. You know, if you want to learn something, write a book about it. By the time I reach fifty-nine I should be ready for fifty-nine pounds.

TACTICAL CHECKLIST

Memorize the following seven points and check your game as you play to make certain you are following the suggestions. If you keep thinking this list intensely, it will soon become an unconscious part of your game. These seven points are easy to learn. They don't require any high degree of co-ordination; all they require is memorization and DOING them. Note that each of the letters in the word TACTICS is the first letter of the key word, so during a set you can check off each letter mentally and thus insure that you are recalling them all.

T Take your time before each service. Think: 1. Feet. 2. Toss. 3. Aim point. 4. Slit. 5. Weight transfer forward. Your service stroke is probably fairly grooved, but it doesn't do you one bit of good if your feet are hastily placed, your toss is hurried or erratic, and you merely hit the ball in the general direction of the opponent's service court. Think before the second serve also. When you've missed your first serve, don't just wind up and flail away for a second muff, as most beginners do. Think and recheck the big five.

A Attack
Whenever the opponent hits you a short, high-bouncing return, hit it aggressively to a *deep* corner and take the net. Make him pass you. Don't get in the habit of hitting an approach shot and then retreating to the baseline again. You just give the opponent another rally chance.

C Crack 'em DEEP
Overhit rather than underhit, or you'll find the opponent running you all over the court. Better a few long drives that go out than giving the opponent all short drives, even though they go in. He'll have you exhausted by the middle of the second set.

T Target early
Pick the spot where you are going to put your return BE-FORE the incoming ball crosses the net. Without target-

ing early, you'll be crosscourting everything to his forehand unconsciously.

I Intensify your effort to return the ball to his backhand corner
Zero in on that back eight-foot square even if you have to lob to get it there.

C Concentrate on the ball
Think ball and watch ball from his racket to your racket. Constantly.

S Scramble fast
Move your feet fast and get into position early, ESPECIALLY ON THE EASY OR NORMAL RETURNS. Too many beginners run hard for the difficult wide returns but loaf when the ball comes right toward them. Move fast on EVERY ball. Get the body out of the way of the ball; pretend you're on a hot plate. Bounce, move early, get set, and then your stroke will feel like Ken Rosewall's.

HANDICAPPING

If you play in a club or another organization that has a challenge ladder system for determining player rating, you may find there is very little "challenging" done, because once the ratings are established the idea stagnates as lesser players assume that challenges are rather fruitless. But there is another ladder that can be set up just for fun. This handicap ladder often makes for much more intermingling of players, and it poses challenges to the top players as well as the lower ones. It works as follows:

First, list all the players in order of rank and divide them into seven equal groups. Players in the first step get 0 handicap. Players in the second step get two points handicap, third step four, fourth step six, and so on to seventh step, which gets a twelve-point handicap. (You may want to revise this later, but it is a good starting place.) The point handicap is for each set played.

A player can challenge any other player, regardless of position above him or below him on the ladder, but once he has played him, he cannot rechallenge for a set period, say, one month. Nor can HE be rechallenged by the other for one month. (Again, these rules can be modified depending on the number and types of players you have.) If he wins he changes places on the ladder with the opponent but keeps his own original handicap. It is another good idea to have this handicap ladder made up by players who volunteer to be in it and have a good sense of humor. Because watch. Let's say a player in the lowest bracket, step 7, with a handicap of twelve points, challenges a player in the top bracket with 0 handicap. They play the first game and the score gets to 30–30. The weak player then uses two of his twelve handicap points to claim the game. The top player begins to see the handwriting on the wall, because if he allows the weaker player to get two points in most games, he, the top player, will lose the set. This means then that he has to stop loafing and make darn certain he gets four points BEFORE his lowly grinning opponent gets two! Of course, the lower guy knows this also, and finds that he can actually loosen up and start going for broke. BECAUSE ALL HE

NEEDS PER GAME IS ONE SMASHER to give his opponent "choke-up-itis." Scoring stays the same, of course, and if the top player gets to 40 and the lower player gets to 30, the lower player would then have to use three chips or points to win that game. One to make it 40–40 and two more for ad and game, so he would probably play the game out, since it would not be wise to waste three chips per game this early in the match when two chips might well take the next game. And the Lord help the top player if the lowly player ever gets to, say, 40–15. The lower player should not use a chip to take the game. He should first try two cannonball serves in the hope of landing one ace and getting the game without using a chip. If he loses the point and the score then is 40–30, he can still use one chip to claim the game. Remember, the lower player gets the same twelve-point handicap in the next set too.

If two lower players meet—say a handicap 10 challenges a handicap 4—they merely subtract four from ten, and the lower player has six points to use at any time during the set. All in all, these matches can be a real challenge to top as well as bottom players. The top player has to concentrate on EVERY point, and if the handicapping has been done reasonably well you will find a sprinkling of lower players near the top of the ladder and a sprinkling of top players farther down the ladder, because the matches will be determined upon who played best within their own capabilities that particular day. On the other hand, if after a couple of months the ladder shows most of the top players on the bottom and most of the lower players at the top, you are overhandicapping. Then try separating the players into six equal groups instead, with no handicap higher than ten. Don't forget either that the real no-handicap ladder must be kept going to place players in the correct step as they improve.

Often the entire level of play of a club goes UP when a handicap ladder is used IF the better players will challenge DOWN the ladder. The weak players rarely challenge a strong player, because they know they don't give him much of a workout. If the top club players get the habit of "challenging" weaker players occasionally on the handicap basis, it helps spread their expertise over the entire range of players. The lower players start concentrating on GETTING THOSE TWO POINTS, instead of feeling, "Well, let's get this over with." And within a year the weaker players are hitting harder, enjoying the game more, and feeling more like part of the club. There is still plenty of time for the top players to play together, and they often find a lot of laughs out of being beaten by a high-handicap player in August who could hardly make a return of serve in June. Then the top player starts yelling good-naturedly that the weaker player has too much handicap. And, of course, the weaker player always has to stand a round of drinks when he gets shifted from a twelve handicap to a ten handicap.

To assist in keeping track of handicap points used up during a match like this, keep a can of old poker chips, or even stones, on the sidelines. The lower player then lays out his handicap in chips stacked by the net post, and as the game progresses he tosses the chips that he used to claim points back in the can whenever the players switch sides. This leaves the correct number of chips still left to be used in plain sight and prevents foulups in keeping track of who used what, when.

If you don't belong to a group, there is another handicap system that varies as the match progresses. It is worked as follows:

First game, no handicap either side. Whoever loses the first game gets fifteen points on the next game, with server starting in advantage court. (If the player who lost the first game wins the second, he wipes out his fifteen-point handicap, and the third game is played even up again.) But say the weaker player loses the second game also, even though he had a fifteen-point lead. He then gets thirty points on the third game, with server starting in the deuce court. If he loses the third game also, he gets forty points on the fourth game, with server starting in the advantage court, and forty is the largest handicap he can get, even though he continues to lose. Now, say, however, that he wins the fourth game. His handicap drops to thirty in the fifth game, and if he wins that, it drops to fifteen in the sixth game, etc. This is a good system to use with your spouse while he or she is developing a game to equal yours. They can see their improvement as their handicap lowers instead of getting smashed every set.

BUILDING A COURT

Do you live way out in the sticks and wish you had a tennis court? Make one. Outside dimensions of a tennis court are thirty-six by seventy-eight feet. Leave twenty-one feet beyond each baseline for backcourt and about six feet on each side of the sideline. Dig this area out to a depth of about four inches as level as you can sight it, with a slope to one side of about four inches to help drainage. Now tamp the dirt down with sledgehammers, rocks, or tampers. All around the outside edge lay on edge two-by-fours (preferably redwood—it doesn't rot) backed up by twelve-inch stakes at six-foot intervals or so, and back them up with dirt. Now have an asphalt company lay in three inches of asphalt with a fine asphalt finish coat, and roll it level with the top edge of the two-by-fours. We made one in our backyard for six hundred dollars that has lasted for twenty years and is still going.

The asphalt takes a week or so to set up, and when it is cured, sift a one-hundred-pound sack of Portland Cement powder all over the court and brush it in well with a broom until the whole area is covered with a thin dust layer of cement powder. Do this just before nightfall and then use a hose or watering can and spray as lightly as possible to fog the entire surface. Try not to let the water run in rivulets, since it will wash away the cement. Just dampen it thoroughly. If there are streaks you can add a bit of powder here and there and broom it back together as you fog. This surface will dry and harden fairly well overnight, but keep it damp the next day with intermittent misting. On a very hot day it may need water every few hours. Keep it damp for about three or four days and the powder and sand particles will have set up in the pits and pores of the asphalt and give you a pretty good gray surface that will not tear up the tennis balls or your knees.

Paint the stripes on with black lacquer or acrylic spray cans. (Don't use oil base or enamel paints, because the oil will eat into the asphalt and curl up the surface under the hot sun.) You must use lacquer or acrylic or you will ruin the court. Lay two six-inch-wide boards about two inches apart on each side of the stripe to be painted and run the spray along the slit between them. The stripes should be painted on the insides of all the dimension lines of the court with the exception of the center divider line for service courts, which is centered on the dimension line.

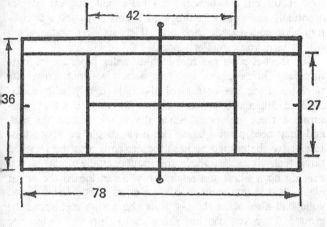

Diagram V

Now, if you don't have the money for an asphalt court you can use the same tamped base but drag in as much as a quarter to a half inch pea gravel, or any gravel you can get for a two-inch drainage base, and tamp that in as hard as you can. Then bring in a few truckloads, or as many boxes as you can get in the old station wagon, of a coarse sand to fill up the spaces between the gravel stones, and tamp that down. Now locate some good clay in the area and fill up the top two inches with the clay, and tamp that down. If you can get a small steamroller and roll it down, it will really give you a tough surface. If your clay is very fine you can brush in some fine sand on the surface just before you roll it to give the surface a little more tooth. Too much will make it too slippery, but the excess can be brushed off with a broom.

For backstops use sixteen-foot redwood four-by-fours sunk

into four-foot-deep holes about nine feet apart. Chicken wire is too light. Use instead the galvanized welded twelve-gauge, rectangular two-inch-by-four-inch openings, fencing that costs about twenty-five dollars for a hundred-foot roll forty-eight inches high. Two rolls will cover both ends. Use galvanized staples and tack it up on the inside of the posts. (If you tack it up on the outside, the balls pull out the staples eventually and your wire drops off.) This gives you a twelve-foot-high backstop at each end, thirty-six feet wide, which will do until you can afford more.

For the net posts use four-inch-diameter pipes set in four-foot-deep holes about two or three feet out from the sidelines. Pack the bottom of the hole tightly with rocks, assorted fill, and a concrete slurry. There is a lot of pressure on these net posts, since the net is pulled up taut, and they need a solid base. The posts should be about four feet above the ground because the net cord must be attached three feet, six inches above the ground at the posts. If you can, rig up a wheel and ratchet so you can loosen the net at night. And if you want to use the court for badminton and volleyball also, make the net posts about nine feet above the ground. Then you can just shove the net up to five feet for badminton or eight feet for volleyball. If you can't afford a net, make one out of heavy knotted twine. You don't have to make the net three feet wide, either. Eighteen inches wide is plenty, because you only need the net from the top of the net cord down a foot so you can tell whether the ball went over or under the net cord. Openings in the net should be small enough so the ball can't fly through. Spraying the completed net with a fabric protective plastic coating will keep it from getting damp and rotting. Or else take it in each night. Ordinary rope, if used as the net cord, will tend to stretch and sag. A nylon cord is better and, if possible, use a quarter-inch steel cable.

For lines on a clay court staple down canvas strips using square staples about two inches wide with three-inch prongs (these can be made out of bent heavy coat hanger wire).

Clay courts have to be babied, and it is standard practice to have a heavy (a four-foot-wide, thousand-pound, or a two-foot-wide, five-hundred-pound) steel drum roller lying off to one side, which everyone uses to roll the court when the surface gets too torn up. Tack a piece of old carpet to a T bar drag, and drag the court with it just ahead of the roller where the worst scuffs are, and you'll have a brand-new surface ready to go.

Try not to place any court in a hollow, since the water collects under it and causes expansion problems. Also try to make certain that the entire court is laid on one type of earth—that is, it is best to have the whole court laid out on solid original soil, or secondly, have it laid out on a fill area. But do not lay it out half on original soil and half on fill, because it will tend to break in half, since the fill settles faster than the original soil or expands and contracts at different rates than the original soil. In general the long axis of the court should be laid out in a north–south direction so you don't get the late-afternoon or early-morning sun directly into your eyes. Got it? You're off!

SPORTSMANSHIP

Much of the philosophy of tennis is predicated upon one thing: the opponents are somewhat equal in ability. Outside of the professional tours and seeded players, however, there are usually great differences among players. The old salts in tennis don't seem to worry much about playing a weaker player; in fact, they seem to enjoy it as much as if they were facing a top pro. On the other hand, there are many players who are in the moderately good class who feel it is beneath them to play anyone a step below them in ability. They will employ the whole gamut of bad manners to avoid playing "lesser" players. And yet those same players are so insensitive that they never realize they, themselves, are "lesser" players to those above them. I have seen three players, "in desperation," invite a fourth to fill in so they could play doubles, and at the end of the first set ask a better player, who happened along, to play the second set and merely leave the first guest sitting on the sidelines without even a thank you. In general, tennis players are pretty good sports, and most of this silly snobbery is found usually among those who start thinking they are pretty sharp players. It is rare among beginners, because they are having such a good time banging the ball around they don't have time to worry about their ego. The top players usually don't worry much about it, because they are too busy working their heads off on the circuit. And if they do play anyone, duffer, intermediate, or club player, they usually beat them all 6–0 anyhow, so they could give a damn one way or the other. So, intermediate young one, beware! When you find yourself holding whispered conversations about another player; trying to avoid playing with anyone but that slick group you played with twice last week; inventing three or four quick excuses if so and so should ask to play . . . you probably think you are better than you are. Why not relax and consider the following:

When you play against a weaker opponent, practice your weakest strokes, or your rush to the net, or your down-the-line shots, etc. You may even try to hit every ball so it bounces just right for your opponent's forehand drive shot and then see if you can beat him anyway by scrambling. Give yourself limitations, and you will find you can have a good match and IMPROVE your own game by seeing how accurately you can place GOOD bounces for your opponent. If you can control that ball, it matters not if you are giving him good bounces, because later on, when you play a tougher opponent, you will have the control to place the bounce where he CAN'T reach them. Right?

In a tournament, however, you should try to win as soon as possible, because you are going to have to play a number of matches. This is no time to play games or feel sorry for the opponent. Tournament players are there for one thing—to see how good they are—and they don't want to be babied. There is another danger when you are ahead 5–0, to feel sorry for an opponent because his girlfriend or family is watching and let him have a game. (Be a good sport, you know.) That one game can be the birth of an awful monster known as confidence, and all of a sudden you realize HE is making that extra point during the deuce-ad games and you are down 5–6 and shaking like a leaf. Being a good sport is not babying someone in a tournament; it is giving him the respect of playing all out and as hard as you can to beat him. Getting beaten 0–6 is the honorable way to go. Most players would rather have the opponent really trying all the way. And this attitude also brings out the best in the weaker man. He learns in a match like this also.

What coaches and good players deplore the most is the fairly good, young player who has an attitude that he is only playing this dolt across the net as a lark until he meets a tougher player. He stifles exaggerated yawns, comments to his buddies on the sidelines, stands straight-legged dangling his racket while waiting for the service, etc. Actually, he is only presenting himself as an ill-mannered boor, and on those occasions when some little bowlegged retriever beats him 6–3 in the second straight set, the bystanders clap and shout for five minutes. Moral: Be a gentleman. Play to win.

I have mentioned the bored player commenting to buddies on the sidelines, the egoist, and the player who loses his temper. There is a fourth type that is by far the worst sport of all. The first three mentioned are irritating, but they are their own worst enemies. This fourth type is the player who deliberately uses a variety of stalls, or minor infractions of the rules, to irritate his opponent or change the tempo of the game in order to win. These stalls are almost always used by players who are behind or who are confronted with a hot winning streak by their opponent. Some even believe it is part of the game, or consider it "colorful" as long as they can get away with it.

Leisurely untying and tying a shoelace and then doing the same on the other shoe between critical points is a dandy way to work up anger in your opponent. Make him pause, seethe, and destroy his service rhythm. Or start toward the court between end change but as soon as your opponent starts walking out into position, stop, examine the strings on your racket, go back to the rack stand, and examine your extra rackets looking carefully at something important, like the label. Then after you're certain your opponent has been standing in the hot sun just long enough to get irritated, and just before the umpire reminds you so politely, "Play must be continuous, Mr. Schlunck," pick up the same racket you were using and walk slowly out into position.

This next stall is the best of all and can be used only by the top players in the world, because who else has linesmen and an umpire to make the game as fair as possible? Your opponent has just hit two hot placements on return of serve. The last one was right on the line, but here's your chance to break your opponent's rhythm. Put your hands on your hips, walk slowly over to where the ball bounced, look down, shake your head, glare at the linesman for eight seconds, and slowly, very slowly (notice that none of these actions are ever done hastily) walk back to the baseline. Look at the heavens, and then with a shake of the head and a shrug of the shoulders, smile wanly at the gallery. The smile is to get the audience back on your side. Implication: "You people understand what we good players have to put up with: incompetent linesmen, weak umpires, tsk. Am I not a courageous figure?" This is almost always good for a ripple of laughter from the spectators who do not play tennis. The part of the gallery made up of tennis players is not laughing. They are thinking, "If I were the umpire I would warn him once, and if he did it again I'd default him come hell or high water."

Throughout the history of tennis, scores of English players and others like Cochet and Von Cramm from the Continent and Budge from America have said time and again that tennis players should respect the calls of linesmen and umpires. The umpire and linesmen should be considered "infallible," and if any errors are made they will cancel each other out over the long run of a match.

Another situation: If a player assumes a call is wrong and in his favor he sometimes "throws" the next point in favor of his opponent (and usually quite obviously). This act is also unsporting. The player has shown by an act like this that he believes he is in a better position to call close balls than the linesmen and better qualified than the umpire to make judgments. The throwing of a point implies that the officials are incompetent, and he, the player, has pre-empted the duties of the officials whose responsibility it is to make certain the game is as fair as possible. If the officials are considered incompetent by the players, then there is always formal recourse through the referee, and the involved linesmen may be replaced or do not have to be asked again. But it should not be the prerogative of one or two players, in the middle of a game, to argue with or insult the appointed officials.

The knowledgeable tennis audience all over the world is incensed at stalls, because the honest player is entitled to his good shots and his hot streaks. When the dishonest player has a hot streak, the honest opponent keeps right on playing "continuously" as the rules request and does not attempt to deprive his opponent of his earned shots or plateaus of action. Thus the stalling tactics of the dishonest players work for injustice in the final scoring.

The most deplorable point to be made against this grandstanding, of top players particularly, is the nationwide prominence given their tournaments. Temper tantrums, thrown rackets, balls smashed against the backstop six feet from a ballboy or into the stands, receiver's partner whirling his racket just before the opponent starts his serve, six-inch footfaults (uncalled), standing over a linesman and glowering at him, are pretty obvious infractions of the rules, or at the very least, disrespect for other human beings. The ballboy might have been hit in the eye. The linesman is made to look like a fool and has very little recourse against Superstar. This behavior is seen on TV, of course, by all upcoming young players. They see this behavior condoned and even smiled at by umpires and therefore are quick to assume that it is their prerogative to use the same tactics to win.

The coaches, umpires, and players who condone these stalling tactics usually refer to them as "temperament." Evidently a word like this salves their consciences. Remarks in tennis interviews like, "Well, we must expect a certain amount of temperament from Schlunck, because he is a very dedicated player and has an intense desire to win" are typical sops, as if no one else has an intense desire to win unless they pout, complain, and stall. In plain language it means, "Schlunck is a brat, and because he can't stand losing honestly, he stalls his opponent's game by petty tricks or pretending to lose his temper." In many regional, national, or world matches, two or three points will determine the difference between winner and loser, and Mr. Schlunck knows very well that all he needs are two or three stalls per match to gain a little edge. He fools nobody but the officials who deny umpires the authority to level point or game penalties consistent with infractions.

Under Rule 30, "Stalling," the umpire is allowed to determine whether stalling is deliberate. If so he should warn the player to stop. "If this does not end it, he should then default him." Actually, within the meaning of the verb default, an umpire (backed by a strong referee) should be able to penalize an erring player a game as well as an entire match. Literally, default applies to any "game, contest, match, or tournament" in most dictionaries. And it is very likely that the original rulemakers intended this to be its interpretation.

However, in late years, with the growth of professional tennis, have come added problems of Superstar, percentage guarantees, and box office, and with it a sort of paralyzing vagueness in the disciplinary part of the rules has been brought on by the unwillingness of tournament managements to back up their field officials in disciplinary actions mainly because of box-office anxieties: "Imagine if Schlunck walked off the court!" What management and officialdom have not had the foresight to consider is the day when Mr. L, Mr. S, Mr. M, and Mr. O, all the honest players, get together and walk out of a big tournament because they are fed up with NONenforcement of rules and ethics.

Tennis officials have considered allowing umpires to levy monetary penalties for rule infractions. This type of penalty would mean very little to the money-making professional, whereas a game or point penalty is much more effective and can also be applied to those players with amateur ratings. However, to date, top officialdom has consented to nothing whatever in the way of minor penalties that would return control of the matches to the umpire again. It may be that some well-respected umpire, backed by a strong-minded, ethical referee, will lay their necks on the block and merely start docking rule violators with game or point penalties on the theory that the original Rule 30 intended for "default" penalties to be applied consistent with the infraction. Everyone seems to be afraid of what would happen. But if the management of an open tournament were behind the referee and umpire in this matter, and the players in the tournament were warned AHEAD of time, I have a hunch nothing would happen except for a big sigh of relief from all involved. And, undoubtedly, an action like this would spark a similar revision in the amateur penalties immediately thereafter also.

If you would like to see umpires in tennis have the same authority umpires have in other sports and help tennis keep its reputation, why not write your opinion to the USLTA and managers of professional circuits?

On the other side of the coin, most intermediate matches and tournaments are played without linesmen or umpire. And the unwritten rule is usually that each side calls the balls as they see them on their side. It is remarkable how the good intermediates ordinarily play everything that bounces near the line, whether it is in or out. Even if the ball lands one or two inches out they ordinarily bang it back and assume it was a good shot. Especially on serves this is very noticeable, and unknowledgeable spectators often exclaim, "Why, that was way out!" There is a good reason for this, however. When a ball is coming fast (and even in intermediate tennis, eighty miles per hour is not uncommon), the receiver has a lot to do besides notice where the bounce was. If he stops each time before he strokes to check the spot where the ball landed he would be missing too many good balls, so he plays ALL the close ones. If the ball is way out, like six or eight inches, it is pretty obvious, and then he just yells "Out!" after he strokes it, or as soon as he can. It is entirely cricket to stroke the ball and then yell "Out!" because otherwise the receiver is being penalized by having to hold back on his stroke to see if it is out and then having it fall in.

Several of the top professional players hit back ALL balls they can reach, whether they are in or not. That way they never miss a close one that the linesman may call in, and as one of them has said, "I get more practice and keep in rhythm by taking them as they come." It is interesting that this type of player never argues with linesmen, accepts all calls, keeps his cool, waits patiently while the staller flaunts his sad manners, and then usually beats the staller anyhow. This is the type of player who is emulated by almost all intermediates. These weaker players bend over backward to call balls good for the opponent. They love the game so much that they'd rather sock the ball than stop the rally just for a lousy point! This is one thought that intermediates can always carry with them: "You may not be a seeded player or in the top ten, but you are playing with some of the best athletes in the world: Those who still consider honorable playing as 'a very essential part of winning.'"

Sportsmanship is also beginning to enter many private tennis clubs by the front door. After ten to fifteen years of some increasing opportunities in business, and particularly education, blacks and other minority groups are beginning to surface in the upper economic levels where they can afford club memberships. And in some areas these minority groups are joining the previous whites-only atmosphere. Integration IS slow. But it does appear, nevertheless, as if some tennis clubs are gradually beginning to jerk themselves out of colonialism into the twentieth century.

ANALYSIS

Below are some examples of errors made by intermediates that can be corrected by intensive thinking and practice. You may note that some of the faults pointed out are listed as causing different problems. "Falling back," for example, may be the cause of a ball hitting the net because you had no weight behind your stroke. But also "falling back" can cause you to hit the ball too long because you are leaning backward and thus tend to hit the ball up too high. The faults are in the form of questions, which you will have to answer for yourself as you analyze your game.

Ball gets too close.

> Spin may be bouncing it toward you.
> Taking too many steps?
> Move your feet faster?

Hits rim of racket.

> Watch contact point?
> Earlier backswing?
> Knees bent?
> Stroking FORWARD or chopping downward?

No power.

> Get shoulder into stroke!
> Leaning into stroke? Or is your body falling sideways?
> Forward knee bent? Or is it straight, and bracing you back from follow-through?
> Hitting ball at end of racket? Overreach a bit.
> Shoulder pivoting? Or only arm swinging?
> Shoulder coming through toward net or falling off to one side?
> Wrist locked?
> Squeezing before contact?
> Letting your back foot swing around? Keep it planted!

Hurried or back on heels.

Watching ball leave opponent's racket?
Backswing before ball crosses net?
Playing too far ahead of baseline?
Giving opponent short returns? Or too-high bounces to forehand?
Using split stop hop before opponent strokes?
When receiving, try shorter backswing and longer follow-through.

Hitting drives long.

Lower aiming slit?
Increase topspin?
Hit three-quarter speed instead of slugging?
Stroke fluid? Or batting ball last few inches before contact?
Racket face perpendicular to ground? Or facing up?
Wrist below racket head?
Falling back while stroking?
Front leg bent?
Lifting head before finishing stroke?

Hitting drives into net.

Move aiming slit higher?
Hit flatter. Less topspin.
Thinking DEEP?
Falling back while stroking?
Forward leg bent?

Forehand drives going out to left.

Contacting ball too soon?
Wrist bent slightly back on contact?
Left foot stepping toward net or out to left?
Stroking with arm only and not pivoting shoulders?
Keeping handle parallel to net on follow-through?
Dragging right shoulder across chest?

Backhand shots slow and high.

Keeping right shoulder LOW?
Racket head following through toward net?
Dragging arm across front of chest?
Bending front knee?
Falling back as stroke?
Racket face too "open" (slanted back at the top)?
Just plain afraid to hit it with vigor?
Early backswing?
Pivoting shoulders extra hard?
Using that left hand to start racket forward?

Hitting net cord on first service.

Contact ball with flat racket BEFORE topspinning it?
Raise aiming slit one foot?
Tossing ball too far in front?
Pushing off with legs may add a bit of topspin.
Serving over your left shoulder?
Wrist snap UP and forward, or forward only?
Tossing ball too high?
Thinking before starting service, or just walking sloppily into it?

And so forth. Analyze your errors as you go. EVERY STROKE!

When analyzing your own game or working with someone else, it is usually necessary to concentrate on specific parts of the stroke as a start. But always try to remember that the parts eventually have to go together, and they should go together smoothly in one coordinated flowing action from split stop through anticipation to footwork and fluid stroking pattern and back to split stop. Ken Rosewall has one of the most classic easy movements in the history of the game. This is probably one of the reasons he can face ten to fifteen opponents in a long, grueling tournament and still come out on top, even though he is not a large man and is in his late thirties. Watch his footwork and his easy-looking stroke and try to emulate them. It helps if you know what standard you are shooting for, and he is an excellent example.

A fluid stroke means that your racket head starts out slowly, gains speed until it is at optimum force on impact, and then flows right on "through" the point of contact. The implication is that you do not flick at the ball by snapping your wrist or bat at the ball with a quick arm movement. This same "fluid" idea can be emphasized also in your footwork and approach to the ball. Coaches often recommend that intermediates use a rhythmic chant such as saying, "back" (when you start your shoulder pivot and backswing), "bounce" (when the ball bounces), "step" (when you plant that front foot), and "swat" (when you contact the ball). When the ball is coming in slowly, the chant goes slowly, like:

"Back . . . . . . bounce . . . . . . step . . . . . . swat."

And when it comes in faster, it may well be:

"Back . . . bounce . . . step . . . swat."

Or even:

"Back, bounce, swat," since the step forward almost coincides with impact. After getting on to it, the intermediate can merely think the rhythm. Even though the cadence of incoming balls varies between fast and slow balls, the intervals between the back, bounce, and swat start relating and help keep the muscle pattern consistent on similar speeds. They help the player's timing—he is not as apt to hit too soon or too late. The rhythm helps conserve energy, particularly in the habit of getting the racket back early enough so the weight of the accelerating racket head does the work instead of constricting biceps.

As every coach knows, it is difficult to analyze yourself on all points. So if you play with someone who is as interested as you are in improving his game, have him team up with you for practice sessions. Now, don't try to coach each other as you rally, because you can't watch the other guy's stroke when you are supposed to be watching the ball. Instead, start off with a pail of forty old balls. Have him hit twenty balls to your forehand, let's say, and watch you as you stroke. He should not attempt to return the ball, just watch you and then hit a second ball, etc. Again, don't have him tell you what he thinks is wrong with your stroke. That is stupid. Neither of you is that competent. Instead, just have him answer one simple checklist question you have chosen, such as: "Did I start my backswing BEFORE the ball crossed the net?" All he has to do then is tell you if you didn't, and keep quiet if you did. For the next twenty balls, "Did I keep my head locked as I stroked?" Then pick up the balls and hit two barrages of twenty balls to him, with him choosing HIS questions.

This is one of the few ways that most intermediates can help effectively. The average player makes a lousy coach at his own level, because he tends to coach the specifics he uses himself and does not have the experience necessary to evaluate and leave alone another intermediate's strong points. So help each other by OBSERVING single checklist points chosen by the "pupil," and don't start coaching each other all over the place with eight rapid-fire suggestions you think are wrong with your coaching partner's approach, stance, swing, head, and follow-through; after two days of this you won't speak to each other again, believe me.

One other point: If you don't believe your "coach's" observations, merely change your chosen checklist question. Don't argue with him! Again, you will lose a friend. I have heard two pupils arguing as follows: "You raised your head." "I did not." "Yes, you did!" "I DID NOT!" The issue at this point becomes a test of who can yell the loudest and who is the superior judge. "The idea of Johnny telling me I raise my head. I can beat him any day in the week!" "That may be correct, Horace, but just because you are the slightly better player doesn't make Johnny's observations any less valuable. In fact, Horace, you DO raise your head occasionally, and if you would realize these drills are meant to help you, not cut you down, your drives would be much less erratic." Now, adults aren't this obvious, but the same thing goes on in our minds when we are asking for criticism from our own peers. We rarely dream of arguing with the professional coach we are paying eight dollars per half hour. So why start arguing with the "coach" you ASKED to help you for free? His observation may be sharper than you think. After all, you have to be thinking of ten or twelve items per stroke, while he only has to watch for ONE. (Even top athletes sometimes have to be shown bad stroking habits by way of movies, because they don't believe what coaches tell them.) He may be correct. Why not start concentrating on that checklist point until he is satisfied you have accomplished it? After all, you chose the question, and if you are so certain he is wrong, why are you practicing? Top players are often much humbler than mediocre players. They are top because they were humble to begin with, whereas the poorer player is often too insecure or arrogant to accept coaching at any level. Learn to take criticism (even from your dad) and you'll become a better player.

The above method of using a pail of balls in units of twenty balls per drill and CONCENTRATING on one checklist question only, in each unit, can be used very successfully when you are teaching your own sons or daughters too. Many fathers realize the problem of trying to teach tennis to their teen-age son particularly. Too often the sessions end in arguments or displays of temper on each side of the net, with Mom finally having to kid the "boys" into making up. But after two or three of these coaching ordeals the old man finally gives up and hopes the kid will get it some other way. The cause of it all is that Dad, in his enthusiasm, usually shovels out too many suggestions at one time and tends to put immediate evaluation on each of the kid's strokes. "No, not that way. This way." "Now, keep your racket face perpendicular." "Step IN to it. No, not toward the ball . . .

toward the NET. Forward." "Don't lean back." "No, no, don't fall backward that way," etc., etc., until son John has it up to the eyeballs, and lashes back in disgust. "I can't do it. I'll never learn all that junk! I don't want to play anymore." Coaches know all of this, because they have gone through it too, before they became good coaches. Good coaches start beginners with simple single suggestions. They make simple corrections by demonstration or quiet praise. They learn to wait a few minutes before evaluating, since they well know that what a kid hears is not translated immediately into smooth physical action. A pupil may make several funny-looking swings and then all of a sudden start correcting himself WITHOUT further coaching. Sensitive coaches go painfully slow and try to get a little fun and play into the game as soon as they can, such as putting a pupil in each service court and having them hit the ball back and forth carefully to each other. And when each team gets six bounces back and forth without missing, they get a cup of orange juice. Thus it becomes a team effort helping each other to maintain the rally, and not a competitive one of who can beat the other just yet.

So here's a suggestion, Dad. BEFORE you go out to practice with No. 1 son, sit down with him in the living room and discuss one stroke for just a few minutes, say the forehand drive. Don't confound him with all twenty-two items in the checklist. Just go through the stroke a few times, showing him the basic step, shoulder pivot, and swing. (For Pete's sake, don't knock over the Chinese vase.) Then tell him you're going to bounce about ten balls to him, and when he hits them, what item does he want you to correct him on? Backswing? Racket perpendicular? Left foot stepping forward? Or what? But only one. O.K.? So you get to the court and do just that. And keep your big mouth closed on all the other items. After ten balls, try him on ten more. He may want to change the checklist item now, or he may not. Let him choose, even if he didn't get anywhere near hitting the darn ball correctly. Let him feel he is doing some of his own training. Now (and this will kill you) let him throw (if he's small) or hit (if he's competent enough) ten balls to YOU and tell YOU whether you raised your head when you made

YOUR forehand stroke (or whatever item you chose to be corrected on). Tell him that he not only helps you, but that it makes him that much more aware of what he's supposed to do. He may know you're kidding a bit, but you can laugh together, and you can raise your head really "booby-like" on one shot to see if he really calls you, etc. Turn about and send the two barrages back at him, and then say, "Well, you think that's enough for one day?" (Always try to end the session while things are going well. YOU be the one to suggest stopping.) He may well say "O.K.," but he more likely will say, "Aw, just one more pail, Dad." And when he says THAT, you've got him hooked. Believe me, those ten-ball barrages become twenty in no time at all, and even though he's not being corrected constantly he starts analyzing his own stroke, learns by criticizing yours, and finally starts playing games such as how many times can WE keep the ball going back and forth on one- or two-bounce hits. "Gee, Mom, Dad and I hit the ball back fifteen times today before Dad missed!" Hm-m-m-mmm.

TEN COMMANDMENTS FOR GROUND STROKES

1. Watch ball come off opponent's stroke.

2. Start shoulder pivot with backswing early.

3. Elbow tucked in slightly.

4. Step into ball toward net with back foot planted and knees bent all the way.

5. Wrist below racket head and SQUEEZE.

6. Think target.

7. Contact ball ahead of torso.

8. Watch contact point a moment AFTER impact.

9. Keep handle and racket head perpendicular to line to target.

10. Long follow-through, with handle of racket staying "parallel to net" as long as possible.

After two or three years of intensive practice you will find yourself hitting much more consistently. At the same time you will be starting to face players who hit the ball harder and more accurately. Below are a few coaching suggestions you can be aware of. See if you can gradually fit them into your advanced game.

1. If you have trouble getting your backhand backswing started forward in time to meet those fast, incoming crosscourts, take up your split stop defensive stance but hold your racket head off to the left (your backhand side) instead of straight out in front. This gives you a little better start on your backhand backswing. (You are usually stronger on your forehand side, so you can afford to borrow from Peter to pay Paul in this case.) Use your left hand to start the backhand stroke forward, but continue to use it FARTHER into the stroke by pushing on the handle until slightly before impact or even into the impact. Thus you can shorten your backswing and still get power into your stroke with less time. And if you do shorten the backswing, then exaggerate and lengthen your follow-through. In fact, this type of stroke is what makes the stroke of a professional look so easy and relaxed. He gets that racket head started forward in correct line, even though he is using only 20 percent or 30 percent of his whole swing before impact, and then exaggerates his follow-through for control. He has ceased to need a long backswing like the little fourteen-year-old girl. In fact, he rarely has time for lengthy windups. He puts the continuity of his stroke into the follow-through.

2. Start considering the angle of the incoming ball when you stroke your drive. After the bounce, is the ball coming UP (on the rise) to meet your racket face? Has it reached its peak? Or has it started on a DOWNWARD course as it reaches your racket face? These different angles may make a difference in the consistency of your drive. Beginners are taught to keep the face of the racket perpen-

dicular to the ground on drives, but the advanced player often makes unconscious adjustments to his racket-face angle. On a ball coming up fast he has to close (advance the top edge of the racket) the face a bit or the ball would take off skyward. On a ball coming downward fast he has to open (advance the bottom edge) the face a bit to prevent the ball from rebounding downward excessively. (See diagram below.)

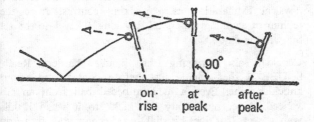

| | on· | at | after |
| | rise | peak | peak |

Diagram W

In either case, the ball is still met with a rising racket face, and in some cases a roll over the top of the ball is necessary to hold a fast-rising ball in court. If you can work your feet fast enough to get to the majority of balls at the same angle, say, "on the rise" or "at peak," then, of course, you have less adjusting to do and can meet more balls with your favorite face angle.

3. The above lines of flight angles are not particularly critical for an intermediate when the balls are coming in slowly, because his stroke overpowers the ball's motion. But when the ball is coming in fast the angle of attack does become more important. Now, if you are a power hitter like Ellsworth Vines was or Roscoe Tanner is and slug everything, the racket usually overpowers any balls, fast or slow. But you have to have pretty good reflexes and coordination for this type of game. Jimmy Connors seems to be a power player of this type too, and if the next generation of players is taller, stronger, faster, and better coordinated than their fathers, the classic tennis strokes and tactics may change somewhat. Better court

surfaces, faster balls, better calibration of string tensions combined with a seven-foot, 220-pound player with unusual coordination who can slug everything for five sets may result in a different ball game. If you are this type of player, great, play it to the hilt. One advantage of hitting the ball hard is that you can, sort of, use the same stroke on every drive. Also, it is a lot of fun, for some men particularly, to sock that ball hard even though they lose the game. It seems to relax them mentally and offers a physical exhilaration as a relaxing contrast from the tedium of shuffling papers all day long. They lose the set but win the day.

4. Consider also gripping the handle harder. Really SQUEEZE that handle just before contact until your knuckles ache. Even a medium-paced ball from an advanced player has plenty of "kick" to it when it hits your racket. If it does hit slightly off center your firm grip is the only insurance against "TILT-YOU-LOSE." Relatively speaking, pros have a hand grip of about 110 pounds, a good "B" player or club player probably about 80 or 90 pounds, with an average woman player perhaps no more than 50 or 60 pounds. Anyone with a strong grip has a great advantage in tennis, because regardless of where the ball hits the strings the racket head will not twist. And if the stroke is fairly consistent, the ball will have that much better chance of going back over the net, not only in the right direction but also with the necessary speed. A weak grip or wrist prevents you from maintaining the LOCKED WRIST all coaches keep yelling about.

There are a few hints to help overcome a weak grip. Remember that little chant a few pages back, "Back . . . bounce . . . step . . . swat"? Well, start substituting the word "squeeze" for the word "swat." This helps in that just before you contact the ball you squeeze that handle a little harder than you have been. It has picked up many a sloppy game, particularly among girl players. Another possibility is to break off about two inches of a wooden matchstick, lay it parallel to your racket handle exactly under the knuckle of either your thumb or forefinger, and tape it in place with a wrap-around of adhesive tape. This slight ridge, then, fits into the wrinkle under the knuckle and acts like a wedge to keep your hand from slipping. In fact, it has always been a mystery to me why the ridges on handle wraps always run around the handle, which is the way the hand slips, instead of parallel to the handle, which would seem to insure a better grip, at least for beginning players. There even have been cases where players cast or whittled the entire handle to fit their own fingers like a grooved glove. This means they have to keep the same grip for backhand as for forehand, but it's a cinch the racket never slipped for them! Also, you can carry around a small sponge rubber ball or an old handball and give it twenty or thirty squeezes as often as you can during the day. Yes, I suppose people will think you are a little crazy, but you can increase your grip strength ten or fifteen pounds within a very short time.

. Forget the score and start taking more chances with the depth of your drives. Overdrive that baseline for six months. See if you can land your bounces about three feet or less from the opponent's baseline instead of the inter- mediates' goal of nine feet. The majority of most inter- mediates' drives or chops land just beyond the service line. If you doubt this, watch two weaker players play a singles match. Note that their feet rarely leave the court itself. It is rare when one of them steps back of the base- line. Stronger players, on the other hand, constantly force the opponent as far back as six or seven feet behind the baseline by placing their drives deep. If you can land your drives deep it prevents your stronger opponent from get- ting a good angle shot at you. And the farther back he has to hit from, the longer time you have to judge the incom- ing ball's trajectory—right?

. Concentrate on your first service even more. Try to get a rhythm of aiming for that slit, SNAPPING THAT WRIST HARD as you follow through LONG. See if you can hit the ball hard enough so that after it bounces in court it hits the backstop before it bounces the second

125

time. Some professionals' first serves hit the backstop seven or eight feet up (watch Roscoe Tanner's serve). If you can develop a hard first service and vary it from backhand to forehand corner, it certainly keeps that opponent on a hot plate wondering where it's coming next. You always have your consistent second serve to back it up. (It is not good to sock that first serve hard until you get through the intermediate stage. Groove your stroke first. Uncontrolled power is useless.)

7. If you do get yourself a hard first service (or a tricky slice), consider starting to the net behind it REGU-LARLY.

Take your muffs for a while. The first hundred muffed volleys and hundred muffed overheads are two hundred practice strikes toward a better game. After six months you'll find you're volleying better and getting maybe one out of three back, then two out of three, etc. (Watch the ball contact the racket like a beetle-browed hawk!)

You may feel that running in after your first serve is a waste of energy. Either the opponent muffs your service and you have taken those two steps toward the net for "nothing," or he does get it back at your ankles and you miss it. So after two or three tries you give it up as a "bad job," stay lazy, and wait on the baseline, where you expend even more energy running back and forth side ways.

There seems to be a built-in complex in tennis players who aren't being formally coached that if it doesn't work the first two or three times they try it, they forget it and return to the old game. As a result they never improve. Don't be one of those.

You must remember that when you're at the net you have a definite psychological as well as tactical advantage. The opponent instinctively tries to keep the ball away from you or at least very low and close to the net. You force him to make his shot in restricted areas. If you are playing an opponent much better than you he will, of course, pass you at will. But if you are playing some one of your own speed, merely crouching aggressive like with racket raised will cause him to make errors, such as missing the sideline shot or lobbing too long or too short. If you have ever faced an opponent who charges up and prowls the net like a cat you'll know how disconcerting that hulk can be. You tend to watch him out of the corner of your eye to see which is the widest area to hit to or which way he is moving, and that alone can cause even the best players moments of indecision. On the other hand, if the opponent stays in the backcourt, there is only your stroke to think of. Why not consider net play as a way to CONSERVE energy? Volleying is fun (like everything else) if you really practice and learn it as well as you did your forehand crosscourt drive. Remember, you don't have to learn to volley—you have to learn to watch the ball contact the strings!

Last, stay cool and keep concentrating. Concentration means watching the ball leave the opponent's racket, watching it come, watching it impact your strings, getting your weight and shoulder into the stroke, moving your feet fast, planning the next stroke, bisecting the area of return, watching the ball leave the opponent's racket, watching it come, watching it impact your strings, watching, watching, watching that BALL!

Concentrating does not mean tensing your muscles, grousing about calls, worrying about how far behind or ahead you are—any of these may be fatal. (When you're behind you choke. When you're ahead you tend to get sloppy.)

THINK POINT.

PLAY FOR THE NEXT POINT BETTER THAN THE PREVIOUS ONE AND YOU CAN'T FAIL TO IMPROVE.

SQUEEZE!

CHECKLISTS

The following checklists are the condensed suggestions IN SEQUENCE for each stroke. Space is left between items so you can write in your own reminders as you better define your game. The number of each item corresponds to the number of the same item in the more expanded form in the previous body of the text.

Look over the checklists just before you practice. Commit four or five items to memory and concentrate on thinking about them EVERY time you stroke. After the stroke, if the ball went awry, think, "What Happened?" See if you can analyze what your error was. For some examples of corrective analysis see the "Analysis" section.

1. Position feet and angle toward aiming point.

2. Shoulders parallel with feet. Nudge left shoulder to right.

3. Start rhythmically.

4. Push up toss accurately.

5. Eyes on contact point AFTER impact.

6. Arc of swing toward aiming point.

7. Aim through slit three feet over net.

8. Transfer weight forward from right to left foot.

9. Legs may be straightened.

10. Fall forward toward aiming point.

11. Strings meet ball flat. Then rip UP and forward.

12. Wrist snap UP and forward AFTER meeting ball flat.

13. Use three-quarter speed for first serve and less for second.

14. If you stay back:
    Singles—split stop at center of baseline.
    Doubles—two strides to open alley and split stop.

15. If you go to the net: Run in to split stop on bisector of
    open field.

TWIST SERVICE

1. Toss more over head and slightly lower.

2. Arch back more.

3. Emphasize UP stroke.

4. Handle parallel with ground on contact.

5. Weight transfer forward emphasized.

6. Place slit four or five feet above net.

7. Follow through to right of body.

133

FLAT SERVICE

1. Use grip "A" in Diagram D.

2. Shift right foot around.

3. Aim direct.

4. Toss higher and farther out in front.

5. Stretch to hit ball flat on "forehead."

6. Aim for slit two feet over net.

7. Lean forward.

8. Wrist snap forward, not down.

SLICE SERVICE

1. Aiming point more to right.

2. Feet and shoulder adjustment to right.

3. Toss farther to right.

4. Contact ball more on right side.

5. Lean into forward motion.

High Chop Serve

1. Starts at shoulder height.

2. Plenty of forward motion.

3. Must go deep.

Low Slice Serve

1. Needs forward motion.

2. Peak over net.

3. Must go deep.

Forehand Drive Serve

1. Feet set as for regular forehand drive.

2. Ball set about waist high off left toe.

3. Moderate topspin stroke.

4. LONG follow-through.

5. Keep head steady. Don't peek.

Low Chop Serve

1. Keep wrist locked.

2. Keep wrist low and below racket head.

3. Bend knees.

4. Aiming slit one foot over net.

5. Place shot deep and AT receiver.

6. Watch contact point. Don't peek.

OVERHEAD

1. If short, let it bounce.

2. Keep ball coming down in front of right eye.

3. Cock racket back early, elbow high.

4. Point at ball with left hand.

5. Keep feet wide apart. Right foot back.

6. Left shoulder toward net.

7. Stroke through ball with FLAT racket.

8. Keep racket head forward of hand on impact.

9. Watch contact point AFTER impact.

10. Aim for large part of court.

11. Keep elbow high followed by moderate wrist snap.

12. Press on first two fingers.

13. Back of hand facing sky at end of stroke.

FOREHAND DRIVE

1. Pick target area.

2. Think deep.

3. Bend knees.

4. Back straight, not rigid or bowed over.

5. Watch ball leave opponent's racket (think target again).

6. Move those feet fast. Weight coming off right foot into left knee.

7. Backswing early.

8. Stroke level, rising slightly.

9. Racket head and arm rising.

10. Keep racket head above wrist.

11. Elbow tucked in during approach to ball?

12. Arm way out on "stretchers"?

13. Left shoulder toward net. Right shoulder follows through FORWARD.

14. Torso as erect as practical.

15. Aim for slit three or four feet over net from baseline, two feet over from midcourt.

16. Contact ball ahead of torso.

17. Eyes locked on impact point.

18. Wrist locked.

19. SQUEEZE grip.

20. Try to keep handle parallel with net as long as possible on follow-through.

21. Hit moderately from midcourt with more topspin.

22. Keep left knee bent until stroke is completed.

APPROACH SHOTS

1. Take your time. Pick target.

2. Shorten your backswing for control.

3. Contact ball at peak of bounce.

4. Contact ball ahead of torso.

5. Hit ball MODERATELY with plenty of follow-through.

6. Watch contact point AFTER impact.

7. Get the point on the NEXT shot.

8. Stroke to target.

9. Move to bisect angle of return.

10. Anticipate AFTER opponent looks away.

RUNNING FOREHAND DRIVE

1. Backswing EARLY. Pivot shoulders.

2. Stroke ball MODERATELY.

3. Plenty of topspin.

4. Steady head (watch impact).

FOREHAND CHOP

1. Backswing early.

2. Racket high at end of backswing.

3. Shorter backswing with flexed elbow.

4. Wrist locked TIGHTLY.

5. Racket moves downhill slightly, mainly forward.

6. Wrist below racket head all the way.

7. Racket face slightly open (top slanted back).

8. Elbow in.

9. Step toward net with left knee bent.

10. Right shoulder punches forward.

11. Meet ball ahead of torso.

12. Watch ball meet racket.

13. Stroke THROUGH ball.

14. Keep handle parallel with net on follow-through.

BACKHAND DRIVE

1. Pick your target.

2. Backswing early. Exaggerate shoulder pivot.

3. Right shoulder low.

4. Left shoulder back forty-five degrees. Back of right shoulder "facing" ball.

5. Lean into stroke toward net.

6. Knees bent all the way.

7. Racket locked at angle with forearm.

8. Lock wrist all the way.

9. Arm straight before contact.

10. Stroke level, rising slightly.

11. Contact ball ahead of torso.

12. Eyes locked after impact (steady head equals steady racket).

13. Racket head above wrist.

14. Racket head rising all the way.

15. Elbow straight and wrist locked during impact.

16. Angle of racket and forearm same at end of stroke.

17. Handle parallel with net at end of stroke.

18. Right shoulder moving toward net (not across front).

1. Pick precise target.

2. Backswing early. Racket high.

3. Racket path mainly forward, downward slightly.

4. Face of racket almost perpendicular to ground.

5. Racket head above wrist.

6. Wrist and elbow locked.

7. No wrist action at end of stroke.

RETURN OF SERVE

1. Choose stroke and target area (lob, chop, or drive?).

2. Back straight.

3. Get ball on rise if you can.

4. Bend knees.

5. Watch ball come off server's racket.

6. Think "backswing," not "ball." Pivot shoulders.

7. Lean into stroke (toward net).

8. Contact ball before it gets even with you.

9. Stroke fluidly through the ball.

10. Racket head higher than wrist.

11. Racket handle kept parallel to net as long as possible follow-through.

VOLLEY

1. Be AGGRESSIVE.

2. Racket out in FRONT.

3. Racket head high.

4. SQUEEZE.

5. Bent knees, but head UP.

6. Keep racket head moving forward.

7. Volley DEEP or low.

8. Get wrist DOWN on low volleys.

9. Lean or STEP into volley.

10. Watch ball contact racket.

11. No follow-through.

12. Be a TIGER.

1. Get low if you have time. Wrist low.

2. Keep top side of racket forward.

3. WATCH ball (most important). Head DOWN.

4. Short follow-through. Blocking action.

1. Watch opponent's stroke and ball coming off racket.

2. Come to split stop. (Watch ball.)

3. Be aggressive. Lean toward ball. Try to volley it.

4. Knees bent. (Watch ball coming down to your racket.)

5. Wrist low and locked. SQUEEZE. (See if you can read trademark on ball.)

6. Watch ball impact racket.

7. Keep knees bent. Don't straighten up.

8. Advance to split stop.

1. At baseline think PEAK slit twenty feet over net.

2. In forecourt think PEAK slit fifteen feet high, behin
   net.

3. Watch ball contact racket face.

4. PUSH slow balls up with flat racket face. Lock wrist.

5. Block-chop fast balls through slit.

O